George Fox Bacon

Northern Maine

Its points of interest and its representative business men, embracing

Houlton, Presque Isle, Caribou, Ft. Fairfield, Danforth, Lincoln,

Mattawamkeag, Winn and Kingman

George Fox Bacon

Northern Maine
*Its points of interest and its representative business men, embracing Houlton,
Presque Isle, Caribou, Ft. Fairfield, Danforth, Lincoln, Mattawamkeag, Winn and
Kingman*

ISBN/EAN: 9783337183233

Printed in Europe, USA, Canada, Australia, Japan

Cover: Foto ©ninafisch / pixelio.de

More available books at **www.hansebooks.com**

ITS

POINTS OF INTEREST,

AND ITS

REPRESENTATIVE BUSINESS MEN,

EMBRACING

HOULTON, PRESQUE ISLE, CARIBOU, FT. FAIRFIELD, DANFORTH,
LINCOLN, MATTAWAMKEAG, WINN AND KINGMAN,

By GEO. F. BACON.

NEWARK, N. J.:
COPYRIGHTED BY
GLENWOOD PUBLISHING COMPANY.
1891.

HOULTON AND ITS POINTS OF INTEREST

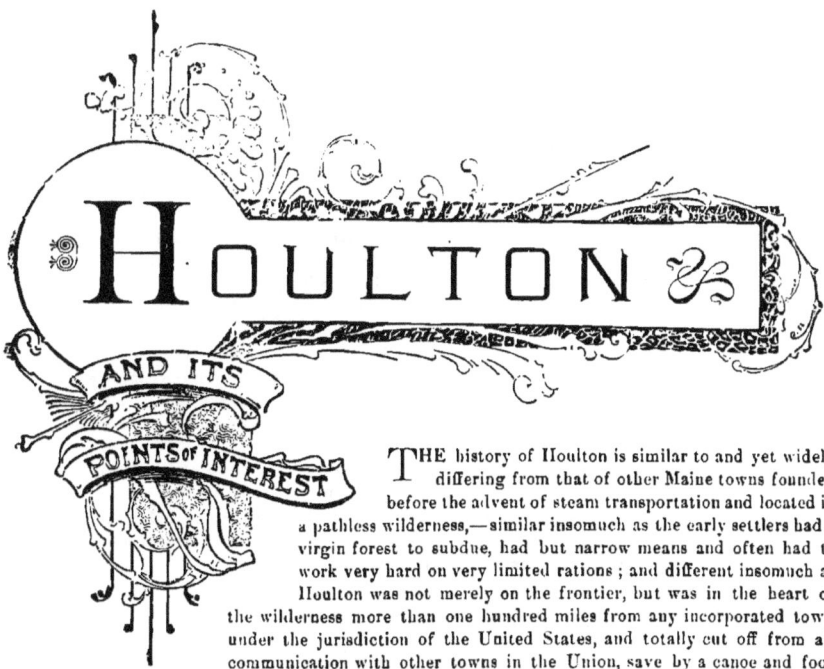

THE history of Houlton is similar to and yet widely differing from that of other Maine towns founded before the advent of steam transportation and located in a pathless wilderness,—similar insomuch as the early settlers had a virgin forest to subdue, had but narrow means and often had to work very hard on very limited rations ; and different insomuch as Houlton was not merely on the frontier, but was in the heart of the wilderness more than one hundred miles from any incorporated town under the jurisdiction of the United States, and totally cut off from all communication with other towns in the Union, save by a canoe and foot journey along rapid streams and through primeval forests ; or by boat from Woodstock, N. B., twelve miles distant through the woods, with no road worthy of the name for years after the work of settlement was begun.

Houlton has been a typical New England community from its inception up to the present time; and this is none the less true because a large portion of the townspeople, past and present, has been and is made up of emigrants from the provinces. Indeed the very birth of the town was due to the New England appreciation of the importance of education; the fulfilling of the conditions of the grant under circumstances which seemed to render such fulfillment practically impossible was due to the same trait; and the ability with which the townspeople have taken advantage of every legitimate means to further their fortunes, and incidentally those of the community as a whole, is also characteristic of New England or "Yankee" methods, and has made Houlton by far the most prosperous and important town in this section of the State.

Owing to imperfect knowledge of the country, the lack of suitable surveying instruments and the inaccuracy of existing maps, all the early grants of land in Maine, and indeed in all New England away from the coast, were very apt to prove uncertain and contradictory as regards their boundaries, so that the pioneers had to take many chances regarding the legality of their holdings and the area of the tract held by each settler. But the grant of the land now occupied by Houlton was exceptionally uncertain, for at the time it was made the location of the boundary between the United States and New Brunswick was in dispute, and as the site of Houlton was in the disputed territory, the original settlers did not know under which government they would eventually be, and not only that but they had every reason to believe that, should the claims of Great Britain be sustained, they would be trespassers, or at least squatters, from a legal point of view, and would thus lose all they had paid for their land, not to mention the cost of improvements. But "nothing venture, nothing win," and there were then as now men who rather relished the element of danger arising from possible future complications.

Not that the original proprietors and settlers of the tract were mere adventurers, or speculators who had merely the furtherance of their own selfish interests in view; on the contrary they were almost without exception devoted to the interests of New Salem Academy, for the maintenance of which the land was granted, and they bought the land because the continuance of the existence of the academy was dependent upon the purchase money, and not because they considered it a profitable speculation. As the history of Houlton is so directly connected with that of New Salem Academy a few words concerning the origin and development of the latter will not be amiss.

"In 1724 a petition was presented to the legislature commencing as follows:

"'Whereas, Salam is a most ancient town of Massachusetts Province, and very much straitened for land, the petitioners pray for a grant in the western part of the province.'—

"The petition was allowed on condition that one lot be reserved for the first settled minister, one for the ministry, and one for a school. Each grantee was required to give a bond of twenty-five pounds to be on the spot, have a house of seven-feet stud and eighteen feet square at least, seven acres of English hay ready to be mowed, and help to build a meeting house and settle a minister within five years. A grandson of Joseph Houlton, of the same name, led the company that emigrated to the assigned location.

"The first result was the town of New Salem in Franklin County, incorporated in 1753, named in honor of the old town from which their leading founder had come. But the people were not satisfied with having merely a school. They must have an academy. They went to work with a will and an academy was established and incorporated in 1795.

"This was the second result. The academy did not flourish to an extent to suit their views and they beset the legislature to grant them a township of land in the woods of Maine, to enable them to endow it. They carried their point, and in 1799 obtained the grant. The effort had been great and great was the rejoicing at its successful issue. But, as bad luck would have it, just at that time land could not be sold at any price. The grant became worthless, and deep and bitter was the disappointment of the people of New Salem. The doom of the academy seemed to be settled and its days numbered and finished.

"But there were men in New Salem who were determined that the academy should be saved. They met in consultation, and, under the lead of still another Joseph Houlton of the same descent, fixed their purpose. They sold or mortgaged their farms, which more than half a century of labor had rendered productive, and which every association and sentiment rendered dear to them. With the money thus raised they bought the granted tract, paying a good price for it. The preservation and endowment of the academy were thus secured, but all benefit from them to themselves or their descendants was wholly relinquished. It was the only way in which the academy could be saved. Some must make the sacrifice and they made it. They packed up bag and baggage, sold off all they could not carry, gathered their families together, bid farewell to the scenes of their birth and childhood, the homes of their life and the fruit of their labor, and started in wagons and carts on their journey to Boston.

"Their location was hundreds of miles distant, far down in the eastern wilderness, and inaccessible from the extremes of settlement at that time on the Penobscot. As the only alternative they embarked in a coasting vessel, went down the Bay of Fundy to St. John, N. B., took a river sloop up to Fredricton—a hundred miles,—got up the river as they could, in barges or canoes, sixty miles further to Woodstock, and turning to the left, struck into the forest until they reached their location.

BIRD'S EYE VIEW OF HOULTON IN 1891.

"The third result of this emigration, in successive generations and stages, from Salem farms is to be seen to-day in a flourishing village, interspersed and surrounded with well cultivated fields, the shire town of the county of Aroostook, in the State of Maine, which bears the name of the leader of this disinterested, self-sacrificing and noble company. Three times was it the lot of this one family to encounter and conquer the difficulties, endure and triumph over the privations and carry through the herculean labors of subduing a rugged wilderness and bringing it to the domain of civilization,— at Salem Village, New Salem and Houlton. It would be difficult to find in all our history a story that more strikingly than this illustrates the elements of the glory and strength of New England zeal for education,—enterprise invigorated by difficulties and powers equal to all emergencies."

The original grant made by the Massachusetts Legislature, June 23, 1799, defined merely the area and not the location of the granted territory, as the following extract will show:

"Resolved, that, in pursuance of a report of a joint committee, which has been accepted by both houses of the Legislature, there be and is hereby granted to the Trustees of the Academy of New Salem, in the county of Hampshire, and their successors forever, one half of a township of land of six miles square, for and to the use of said Academy, to be laid out and assigned by the committee for the sale of eastern lands in some of the unappropriated lands in the district of Maine belonging to this Commonwealth, excepting all lands within six miles of the Penobscot river."

Nearly six years elapsed before the location of the grant was established by the act of John Bead and Peleg Coffin, who, as duly authorized agents of the Commonwealth, "did convey and confirm unto the trustees of New Salem Academy and their successors, to be by them holden, in their corporate capacity, for the use of said Academy, half a township of land lying in county of Washington, containing 11,520 acres, equal to half a township of the contents of six miles square, as the same was surveyed by Park Holland, Esquire, in the year 1801, bounded as follows, viz : beginning at the northeast corner of Groton Academy lands, and running from thence north three miles to a stake and stones."

The township as defined above was conveyed to the academy trustees February 21, 1805, and June 1, 1810, a committee appointed by the trustees conveyed all the rights in and title to the premises "for a valuable consideration paid said trustees, to Aaron Putnam, one-eighth part thereof; to Varney Pierce, one-eighth part thereof; to Joseph Houlton, one-fifth part thereof; to John Putnam, one-tenth part thereof; to Joshua Putnam, one-tenth part thereof; to Rufus Cowles, one-tenth part thereof; to John Chamberlain, one-tenth part thereof ; to William Bowman, one-twentieth part thereof; to Consider Hastings, one-twentieth part thereof; and to Thomas Powers, one-twentieth part thereof." These ten grantees were described as regards residence and occupation as follows:

Aaron Putnam, on the premises, Yeoman.
Varney Pierce, of New Salem, Esquire.
Joseph Houlton, on the premises, Esquire.
John Putnam, of New Salem, Gentleman.
Joshua Putnam, of New Salem, Yeoman.
Rufus Cowles, of Amherst, Physician.
John Chamberlain, of New Salem, Yeoman.
William Bowman, of Hadley, Yeoman.
Consider Hastings, of New Salem, Gentleman.
Thomas Powers, of Greenwich, Esquire.

It will be seen from the above that but two of the proprietors, Aaron Putnam and Joseph Houlton, were settlers at the time the deed was drawn up, and with the exception of Joshua Putnam, who took up his residence at Houlton shortly afterward, none of the remaining proprietors became residents.

One of the conditions of the grant was that at least six families should be settled upon the lands within five years, and it was this condition that very nearly brought about a forfeiture of the property, for it was placed on the market at a most unpropitious time, as the opening of the present century found business in a very dull condition, the people impoverished by the Revolution, our relations with France so strained as to make war seem almost inevitable, while our relations with England were almost equally unfavorable and finally culminated in the war of 1812. Add to these deterring circumstances the fact that the tide of immigration had already set westward, and it will be seen that the chances of finding men of property to buy and settle a tract in the remote eastern wilderness were so small as to be hardly worthy of consideration from a commercial point of view, and indeed had there been no other incentive than that of possible pecuniary profit the grant would unquestionably have been allowed to lapse. But the purchasers were friends of the academy who bought the property with the idea of finding settlers and thus consummating the grant; they paying no money to the trustees when the purchase was made but waiting until they could dispose of their shares to actual settlers. But no such disposition could be made, no moneyed settlers could be found, and with the passage of time it became evident that decisive action must at once be taken, and the question of the continuance of the academy settled for good and all, for its affairs had reached a stage where financial aid was absolutely indispensable. It is impossible to point out with any degree of certainty the person or persons to whom the saving of the grant is due, or rather who found the key to the deadlock upon all progress in the matter which had so jeopardized the Academy. Some historical students give the credit to Joseph Houlton, others to Mrs. Lydia Trask Putnam, mother of one of the purchasers and very prominently identified with Houlton's settlement and development, while still others believe that the course of action finally adopted was not due to suggestions received from any one person but was the outcome of the assembled wisdom of the proprietors. At all events, it is certain that the grantees mentioned in the deed made up the sum of $5,000, by sale of their farms and by other means, and paid it over to the academy, and that just before the five years expired the required number of families settled upon the grant. From this time the work of settlement

MAIN STREET, LOOKING WEST IN 1891.

went steadily on, although slowly. Joseph Houlton built a rough grist-mill in 1808, for the accommodation of all who chose to use it, and few there were who did not, for otherwise they must use hand mills or travel to far-off Fredericton. September 5th, 1809, is memorable as the date of the first petition for the incorporation of Houlton as a town, but the prayer was unavailing, as was also a similar one made eight years later. The settlement was organized as a plantation April 21, 1826, and in 1831 Houlton was duly incorporated as a town, the first town meeting being held April 11th of that year.

Several years before, the general government had made Houlton a military post and it is hardly possible to overestimate the good effect this action had upon the community, for not only did it make life and property more secure, but caused a great deal of money to be paid out for supplies and for wages; the outlay amounting to several thousand dollars a month for a long time, and being distributed almost entirely among residents of Houlton. The reason for the establishment of a military post here was the exposed situation of the town and the uncertainty as to the boundary line between this country and the British possessions. There was a garrison at Fredericton and desertions from it were frequent, as the service was hard, the pay miserable, and many of the soldiers had been impressed or at least enlisted when drunk and hence felt no scruples about deserting at the first opportunity. It was by no means uncommon for American citizens to be enticed to Woodstock and to be made intoxicated, after which they were offered a glass of liquor "in the king's name" and a piece of money, "the king's shilling," was slipped into their hand. From an English point of view this was a legal enlistment, and the luckless drunkard would awake to find himself in the guard house and "bound to serve his majesty." Of course the residents of Houlton suffered from such practices, and were no lovers of the government that sanctioned them, but they could do nothing, even when corporal's guards seeking deserters visited the town, which of course they had no legal right to do. But although offering no active resistance, the townspeople still resisted most effectively in their own way, for it was quite common for deserters to throw themselves upon the protection of the Houlton settlers, and such deserters were never given up but were secreted until an opportunity arrived to smuggle them out of town to Bangor or some other town so far from the frontier that recapture was impossible.

The ending of this condition of affairs was brought about by a Quaker, Jonah Dunn, who came to Houlton in 1826. He at once perceived the abuse of power by the English soldiery, and in the most approved American fashion began to work up public sentiment throughout the country by writing to the newspapers. He caused a petition to be drawn up in 1827, and presented to Congress the following winter, and the necessary act was passed and appropriation made to enable the stars and stripes to wave over Houlton, backed by a force that would ensure their being respected, and secure to every citizen that "life, liberty and the pursuit of happiness" that the Declaration of Independence says is his due.

NICKERSON LAKE, NEAR HOULTON.

The precise date of the arrival of the Federal soldiers at Houlton is uncertain, but the records show several sales of land by Joseph Houlton to the United States in 1828, and the national forces arrived about the middle of that year, Company C, Second U. S. Infantry, under command of Lieut. J. S. Gallagher reaching town some time in June. It is unnecessary to say that the soldiers received a hearty welcome for they were hailed by the townspeople as their deliverers from the long series of petty persecutions and insults they had received from the English, and such indeed they were, for with their coming ended all visits of hostile "corporal's guards," as John Bull had learned to have a wholesome respect for the stars and stripes when backed by anything approaching an adequate force, and the simple fact that Houlton had become a military post so sharpened the perceptions of the Fredericton garrison that they never had difficulty afterward in remembering that the town was outside their jurisdiction.

Company C had left Bangor in connection with three other companies of the same regiment but arrived at Houlton alone as the other companies were ordered to accompany the military stores which were being transported to Houlton by contractors. The task of transporting the stores proved far more difficult than had been anticipated for no roads existed where there were supposed to be some, and the work of making roads passable for heavy military stores proved much more serious than the government had been led to believe. There was said to be a road from the East Branch of the Mattawamkeag River, and the chief reason for the assignment of the three companies before referred to was to employ them in the repairing of that road ; but the event proved that the work was that of building, not repairing, and the arrival of the stores was thereby greatly delayed. Major N. S. Clarke, the commanding officer of the four companies, reached Houlton in August, 1828, and took command there in place of Lieutenant Gallagher, who was ordered to Bangor and connected with the depot and recruiting station there.

By letters written by Major Clarke it appears that the question of stores and supplies for the use of the detachment during the rapidly approaching winter was the most important one that engaged his attention, and he suggested to the authorities at Washington that a change be made in the mode of delivery, an extract from a letter to the Commissary General of Subsistence, dated August 25, 1828, reading as follows :

"The idea has suggested itself that the residue of the annual supply of substinence stores now on its way to Bangor from New York, intended for this command, might be delivered at once at the post by contract, if the contractors should ship them immediately at Bangor to St. John, in the Province of New Brunswick, provided the Revenue Laws of that Province did not interpose too great obstacles.

MARKET SQUARE, WESTERN VIEW, IN 1891.

I very much fear, so dilatory and inefficient have been the arrangements of the contractors for transportation upon the Mattawamkeag, that a partial failure in the delivery of the stores, already on the way to Houlton, may take place. Besides they have been so badly handled, and so much exposed to the unusual rains of the present season that I also fear that much of the flour will be found to be damaged. Under these circumstances, in order to meet any unfortunate contingency, I respectfully suggest to you the propriety of furnishing Lt. Smith with authority and funds to make purchases in case of need."

While the three other companies were kept hard at work all through the summer of 1828 road-building, Company C, which "held the fort" at Houlton, was by no means idle but was actively employed building barracks and preparing the grounds for the military post. Many citizens were also employed in this work, the monthly pay roll for such help ranging from $1,500 to $1,800, but with all this force the task was by no means easy of accomplishment, especially the preparation of the parade ground which called for a great deal of blasting as portions of a great ledge had to be removed. In fact, so much was there to do that the barracks were not sufficiently advanced in building to receive all the soldiers, and a portion of the command therefore passed the winter under canvas, while the officers remained at Mr. Houlton's house. The companies which had been employed at road-building reached Houlton September 29, 1828, and even then all the stores had not arrived, some of the supplies and nearly all the clothing being literally stranded on the way, for they had to be temporarily abandoned owing to lack of water. But enough had been done to ensure the occupancy of the post during the coming winter at least ; there was no doubt that the soldiers had "come to stay," and with their coming ended all trouble from deserters and their pursuers, while money was plenty, work was abundant, and in short the settlement was fairly entered upon an unprecedented era of prosperity. During the winter of 1828-29 the work of road-making was continued, one force cutting out a way through the forest towards Mars Hill and another improving the road to Bangor, but experience made it clear that the conditions were such as to render it unadvisable to attempt the construction of a permanent turnpike road by soldier labor, and the fine military road which was eventually built from the north. of the Mattawamkeag straight through to the barracks was constructed under contract by civilians. It was practically finished by the winter of 1832 and was regarded as a model of perfection, as indeed it was in comparison with other Maine roads at that time. In 1836 the soldiers began building a road from the barracks toward the Province, aided by civilians with teams, and the work was very well done. Every spring the military roads were scientifically repaired and while controlled by the Federal

THE NEW GRAMMAR SCHOOL.

authorities they improved from year to year, but after being surrendered to the local authorities they were neglected, especially after the building of the railways. The result of this short-sighted policy is evident in the very inferior condition of the roads at present, but of late years there has been a growing tendency to improve our New England country roads and it is probable that the original efficiency of some of these military roads will be restored before a great while.

The detachment of the Second Infantry remained at Houlton until the latter part of 1838, when it was relieved by several companies of the First Artillery under command of Major R. M. Kirby, who arrived here just in time to become quite a prominent figure in the so-called "Aroostook war" which commenced early in 1839. This "war" was brought about by the uncertainty as to the boundary between Maine and the Province of New Brunswick and the hot-headedness of private citizens on both sides of the border; they not being content to await the action of their respective governments but taking the law into their own hands and seizing parties whom they detected cutting wood on the wrong side of the line as the self-constituted judges understood it. Large forces of militia were enrolled in Maine and also in New Brunswick, and at one time the Commander at Houlton was called upon for aid, but he refused to afford it and his refusal was thoroughly endorsed by his superior officers. As both the Federal and the English governments were desirous of a peaceful solution of the question of boundary they discouraged all violence, and after some eight weeks of fervid excitement the "war" ended as informally as it had begun and the boundary question was answered for good and all. Its settlement was in one sense a very unfortunate thing for Houlton for it ended the necessity of maintaining a military post there and the withdrawal of the soldiers was a serious blow to the town.

The post was evacuated in 1845 and hard times followed, for even a much larger town would have suffered from the sudden withdrawal of so great a proportion of its population. Valuation of all property sunk very low and great inconvenience was experienced before the community adapted itself to the changed conditions, but still the settlement slowly increased and with the progress of time quite a measure of prosperity was enjoyed, but the busy, rich and handsome Houlton of to-day is the result of the railway facilities enjoyed and it was not until these were provided that the great possibilities of

RICKER CLASSICAL INSTITUTE.

the town were made manifest. Houlton was first reached by a railway in 1870, but had previously profited from the building of an iron road, for the New Brunswick and Canada railroad had been completed from St. Andrews to the Woodstock road, five miles from Houlton, in 1862, and the military road furnished connection with the latter town, a large traffic being carried on over it. The European and North American railway was begun in 1868 and completed to Vanceboro in November, 1871, connection for Houlton and Woodstock being made six miles east of Vanceboro at McAdam junction. Of course the opening of direct railway communication from Bangor to Houlton and the Provinces was a grand good thing for Houlton's business interests, and although the railway companies have in some instances failed owing to lack of capital, etc., affairs in Houlton have fairly "boomed" from the first. Of course the town is interested in having the facilities as perfect as possible, and these have been wonderfully improved of late years, combinations having been effected which guarantee frequent, reliable and generally satisfactory service. Houlton is now but four hours from tide water open throughout the year; but fourteen hours from Boston and seventeen hours from Montreal; and direct daily communication is furnished with that city and the west, besides several daily trains to all points in New England and the Southern and Middle States.

"The smartest village in the smartest town, in the smartest county, in the biggest of the New England States," is the way in which an enthusiastic "drummer" describes the village of Houlton as it exists at the present time, and notwithstanding the free use of superlatives there is more truth than poetry in the description, as will be made evident by analysis, for there is no doubt that Houlton village is the smartest in the township ; there is no doubt that Houlton town is the most prosperous and important town in the county ; there is no doubt that Aroostook county has prospered more and made greater gains during the past decade than any other county in the State and there is no doubt that Maine is the biggest and one of the most enterprising of the New England States. Houlton is most emphatically the metropolis of the frontier and is likely to ever remain so, at all events as long as its advantages of location are supplemented so effectively as they now are by the enterprise and reliability of the local business men. The town is at once a depot and a distributing centre, for supplies are received here from all points for distribution among the residents of the section, and it is from here that the great bulk of the superior produce raised on the exceptionally fertile lands in Houlton and adjacent towns is shipped to the many near and distant points where it is known and valued. The numerous, large frost-proof potato houses clustered about the railway station afford a hint concerning the importance of the trade in this standard vegetable, and indicate by their great capacity that the claim that the potatoes raised in this section are the best and most popular in the country is fully justified by the facts. Houlton is located wholly upon the slate lands of the St. John, it being the first town measuring from the coast to be so located, and its soil possesses all the fertility and other virtues which make this section rank with the most productive farming counties in New England. There is but little surface stone, the soil is the bright yellow loam characteristic of the St. John slate lands, and expert judges say that, acre for acre, the land in Houlton is fully equal to that of any other town in this region. The township is well-watered, and is divided into two parts substantially equal in size by Meduxnekeag River, which flows through it in a northeasterly direction from the southwest corner. A branch of the same stream enters at the northwest corner, making a junction with the river proper at a point approximating the centre of the town and at the head of the mill pond. The surface of the township is agreeably varied, from the southern line nearly half way to the northern boundary being high land which reaches to within a mile and a half of the eastern line ; and a huge ridge or " horseback " extends along the western part of the town, penetrated by streams and highways. The excellence of the soil has caused the removal of nearly all the forest growth but still there is no dearth of trees, the margins of the fields being strongly marked by them, and even the village itself being abundantly supplied, for many noble shade trees line the highways and go far to substantiate Houlton's claim as one of the most beautiful towns in the State. And this claim is also supported by the various elegant private residences scattered about the village and town, nearly all of which stand in the midst of finely arranged and well-kept grounds, and are surrounded by velvety lawns or spreading shade trees, or tastefully designed flower beds. Nor are these adornments confined to the estates of the wealthy or neutralized by the close proximity of the shabby, neglected dwellings, rank grass lands and tangled shrubbery, far too common in some of our New England villages, on the contrary, neatness, taste and care are as conspicuous in the appearance of the smaller cottages as in that of the stately mansions, and a close and experienced observer could not make a tour of Houlton without being convinced that its population was intelligent, public-spirited, prosperous and contented ; for neatly and tastefully kept homes show more conclusively than columns of statistics could that the community in which they are located is enlightened and thriving. Houlton's handsome, elaborate and costly public buildings also add materially to the beauty of the town, the Ricker Classical Institute (a cut of which is printed on page 11), being especially picturesque. The court house, jail building and the Episcopal church (illustrated on page 13), are also structures which are no less beautiful than useful, and indeed there is no other town of no greater population in which natural beauties are more adequately supplemented by the work of the architect and builder. It has often been said that we Americans are so eager in our pursuit of the "mighty dollar" that we have no appreciation of the beautiful and regard everything from a strictly utilitarian stand-point. That may have been the case in the remote past but it is far from being so to-day, and no stronger proof of this could be given than that afforded by the fact that the residents of Houlton—business-like, progressive and industrious as they are, and having profitable employment for all their capital in the extension of their private enterprises—still vote large sums for handsome public buildings, erect fine residences, maintain ornamental grounds and in short show in many ways that enterprise and thrift are by no means incompatible with an appreciation of the beautiful.

Being the shire town of Aroostook County, Houlton of course contains the County Court House. This is quite an elaborate building, erected thirty-odd years ago and costing $35,000. It has a mansard roof, cupola and bell; and here is located the town clock,—a recent gift to the town from public-spirited citizens.

Manufacturing is extensively carried on, the more important products being starch, lumber, machinery and iron work in general including castings, builder's finish, carriages and sleighs. Very large and finely equipped bark extract works are successfully carried on, and slaughtering is also a very

COURT HOUSE, JAIL BUILDING AND EPISCOPAL CHURCH.

important local industry. Woolen goods are quite largely produced and corn meal, etc., are also manufactured. But it is as a trade centre that Houlton excels, and the local stores and warehouses would do credit, in many cases, to a town of much greater population. A building known as the Brick Block contains eight large stores and numerous offices on the upper floor. This structure occupies the site of a number of buildings destroyed during a very destructive fire in 1884, and furnishes an exemplification of the saying "it's an ill wind that blows nobody good" for its existence is due to that conflagration and the block is a credit to architect, builder, owner and community and furnishes a model of what the business edifices of the future Houlton are to resemble. The stores are very high studded, are equipped with great plate glass window panes, are heavily stocked, brilliantly illuminated by electricity, and in short are well calculated to make the visiting stranger who had deemed Houlton a "back-woods town" rub his eyes in astonishment, and wonder if he had not been suddenly transported to Portland or Bangor. And the best of it is, the very favorable impression made by the exterior appearance of Houlton's leading stores is sure to be confirmed and deepened by an examination of the goods and prices and by familiarity with the methods of local merchants. Strangers sometimes wonder that Houlton should be so popular as a purchasing centre, even after making due allowance for its advantages of location, but this wonder never survives a visit to the town and an investigation of the inducements offered for the simple reason that it speedily becomes apparent that these inducements are unequalled elsewhere. No other town in the State can compare with Houlton as a purchasing centre so far as the residents of the country for miles around are concerned, and this is due not alone to superior railway facilities but largely to the enterprise and liberality and ability of those doing business in town. Such a place as Houlton naturally attracts the most progressive traders from other sections, for such men of course "know a good thing when they see it" and are quick to grasp the possibilities of trade in the metropolis of the frontier. The field is well occupied and hence competition is keen and close, but it is almost without exception not only good-natured but strictly honorable, and goods bought from Houlton dealers are practically certain to prove as represented. The excellent banking facilities are second only to the railway facilities in aiding local merchants to carry on business to the best possible advantage, and the result of the combination of favorable conditions brought about of late years is to be seen by a comparison of Houlton prices with those quoted on similar goods in Portland, Bangor and other cities,—such a comparison being by no means unfavorable to our local merchants.

The County Jail is another notable building, and is ornamental as well as useful, although utility was given the first place in its construction. It is a new edifice, cost $27,000 and is very finely arranged and suitably finished. Houlton has always been liberal in the support of schools, as it is fitting a town should be that owes its origin to the New England appreciation of the importance of education. The new Grammar School House is a substantial and handsome brick edifice, erected at a cost of $15,000 and comparing favorably with any school building of similar grade in Maine. Houlton offers especial inducements as a place of residence from an educational point of view, the town containing an Institute which has an enviable and thoroughly deserved reputation for efficiency. Its grounds are spacious and well-arranged and the buildings are large and extremely well-equipped, more than $35,000 having lately been expended on them. There are some beautiful church edifices in town and some elegant private residences, including several old mansion houses and various buildings recently erected and embodying the most advanced ideas of dwelling house architecture. The population of the town is rapidly and steadily increasing as its many advantages as a place. of residence attract many emigrants from the Provinces as well as many enterprising people from Maine and New England in general. Although in one sense of the word remote, Houlton is by no means inaccessible, it being more easily and quickly reached than many towns which lie much farther from the frontier, and it is an impressive fact that Bangor can now be more speedily and easily reached from Houlton than Woodstock could for a number of years following the town's settlement. The mail and telegraph services are very good and the same may be said of the express service, this having been materially improved of late years. Freight rates to and from the town are very satisfactory, and there is good reason to believe that the manufacturing interests of this section are destined to develop very considerably in the near future. Great enterprise is shown in catering to local needs, there being a water company which supplies the village with water of excellent quality at favorable rates ; and the electric light service is also comprehensive, reliable and popular. A sewerage company has taken hold of the important work of drainage and although the system is not complete, enough has been done to show the easy practicability of providing sewerage for double the present population of the village at comparatively small expense. Possessing a healthful and beautiful location, pure air, pure water, good drainage, excellent schools and churches, exceptionally good railway facilities, an industrious and enterprising population and a most excellent reputation as a trade centre, Houlton certainly offers an unusual if not unique combination of advantages as a place of residence, and at its present rate of growth it will soon become worthy of an even more important title than it now holds by right of conquest,—that of Metropolis of the Frontier.

Representative Business Men of Houlton, Me.

BRADFORD, GENTLE & LUDWIG, Insurance Agents, Houlton, Me.—As the amount of insurable property in Houlton and vicinity is not only already large, out is constantly and rapidly increasing, there is naturally a brisk demand for dependable insurance at fair rates, and this demand is most efficiently and satisfactorily catered to by Messrs. Bradford, Gentle & Ludwig, who as a firm and as individuals represent many of the strongest insurance companies in the world, and are prepared to execute commissions promptly and at the lowest rates consistent with positive protection. The firm was organized in 1888, and consists of Mr. J. H. Bradford, a native of Auburn, Me., Mr. George S. Gentle, a native of New Brunswick, and Mr. L. O. Ludwig, a native of Waldoboro, Me. They represent the Northern Assurance Co. of London, the American Insurance Co. of Boston, and the Insurance Co. of North America of Philadelphia. Mr. Bradford represents the Ætna Insurance Co., Hartford ; Hartford Insurance Co., Hartford ; Ætna Life Insurance Co., Hartford ; Pennsylvania Insurance Co., Philadelphia ; First National Insurance Co., Worcester ; Royal Insurance Co., Liverpool. Mr. Gentle represents the Royal Insurance Co., Liverpool ; Employers' Liability (accident), London ; Pennsylvania Insurance Co., Philadelphia ; Traders' Insurance Co., Chicago ; Granite State Insurance Co., New Hampshire. Mr. Bradford carries on a private banking business including the reception of deposits, the payment and collection of drafts, etc., and Mr. Gentle is interested in the purchase, sale and exchange of real estate. Taken as a whole, the facilities offered by Messrs. Bradford, Gentle & Ludwig, associated and individually, are of great importance and form an important factor in the sum of the advantages possessed by Houlton as a business centre.

HOULTON FOUNDRY AND MACHINE Shop ; Shingle Machines, Gang Lath Saws, Rotary Mills, Wood Cutters, Stoves and Plows; manufacturers of the Celebrated "Getchell" Patent Horse Hoe; all Kinds of Machinery Promptly Repaired; dealer in Rubber and Leather Belting and Mill Supplies, Waldo G. Brown, Houlton, Me.—The productions of the Houlton Foundry and Machine Shop are so well and favorably known throughout this section that no detailed mention of them is necessary, suffice it to say, they are unsurpassed for efficiency of design and excellence of material and workmanship, and in some respects are unequalled for everyday practical use. They include shingle machines, gang lath saws, rotary mills, wood cutters, stoves and plows, together with the famous "Getchell" patent horse hoe, and can be furnished at short notice and moderate rates. Spacious and well-arranged premises are utilized and they are fitted up with improved machinery driven by steam-power; every facility for the prompt repairing of all kinds of machinery being at hand, and general machine work being done in a superior manner at short notice. The proprietor and manager, Mr. Waldo G. Brown, is agent for Henry Disston & Sons' and Simonds Manufacturing Co.'s mill, circular and drag saws, and deals in rubber and leather belting and mill supplies of all kinds. He also deals extensively in general hardware, farming tools, paints, oils, glass, bar iron and steel, pumps, wrought iron pipe, steam fittings and plumber's goods, occupying a handsome and spacious store at No. 52 Main street, and adjacent storehouses. This store is one of the largest in the State and is most admirably equipped with modern improvements to facilitate the handling of the immense stock carried. Mr. Brown is a native of Haynesville, Me., and has carried on his present business since 1883 He is engaged also in the manufacture of starch, but in spite of the extent and variety of his enterprises gives them all close personal attention and maintains the service at a high standard of efficiency.

E. WOODBURY & CO., wholesale and retail dealers in Groceries, Provisions, etc., Mechanic Street, Houlton. Me.—Very few men are engaged in active business for half a century, and the number of those who carry on one certain enterprise for that length of time is so small that when a case is met with it can hardly be given too prominent mention, but even were such not the fact we would still be justified in ascribing to Mr. Eben Woodbury a leading position in this review of Houlton's prominent business men, for no man in the town is more universally known and highly esteemed or is a more truly representative citizen in every sense of the word. He is a native of Durham, Me , and began operations as a dealer in groceries, etc., more than fifty years ago, since which time he has had various partners In 1889 he became associated with Mr. John C. McIntyre, under the firm-name of E. Woodbury & Co. Mr. McIntyre is a native of New Brunswick, and has gained a most enviable reputation throughout this section by his accommodating and straightforward methods. Mr. McIntyre is agent for the Am. Ex. Co , a position he has held a number of years, and is also Western ticket agent for the Grand Trunk and Erie railroads. The firm occupy spacious premises on Mechanic street, and deal at both wholesale and retail in groceries, provisions, etc., carrying a large stock, quoting low prices, and assuring prompt service by the employment of four assistants. Mr. Woodbury is the present postmaster of Houlton, which position he has held through several terms. He has held various other important offices, including that of State representative.

FRED VERPLAST, dealer in Boots, Shoes, Hats, Caps, Clothing, etc.; strictly one price; Corner Main and Court Streets, Houlton, Me.—Much time and trouble and no little money may often be saved by purchasing an entire outfit at one place, and we can certainly give such of our readers as are contemplating the purchase of an outfit of clothing no better advice than to call at the establishment conducted by Mr. Fred Verplast, for he carries a complete line of boots, shoes, hats, caps, clothing, etc., and has but ONE PRICE. Mr. Verplast not only handles absolutely dependable goods, but quotes absolutely bottom prices. He is a native of Bangor, Me., and is widely and favorably known throughout Houlton and vicinity. The business with which he is now identified was founded by him in 1889. The patronage is steadily increasing under his skillful management, and the public have long since learned that all representations made at this store can be implicitly relied upon. Besides carrying a full line of staple goods and styles, Mr Verplast offers many of the latest fashionable novelties, and those who like to feel that they are fully "up to the times" in the matter of dress, will appreciate his policy in this respect. Boots and shoes, hats and caps, as well as clothing for either working or dress wear may be bought to excellent advantage of Mr. Fred Verplast, at the corner of Main and Court streets, Houlton, Me.

S. D. AMAZEEN, Barber; Violins and Strings, Violin Fixtures of all kinds; Razors, Brushes and Soaps. Razors Concaved and Honed, No. 15 Market Square, Houlton, Me.—The eminent degree of success attained by the enterprise carried on by Mr. S. D. Amazeen, at No. 15 Market square, is not the result of luck and chance by any manner of means, but has been honestly worked for and is honestly deserved. Mr. Amazeen, who is a native of Exeter, Me., established the business in Houlton in 1871, under the firm name of Amazeen & Hallett. He is a barber and is thoroughly conversant with his business in all its branches. He also carries in stock, razors, brushes, and soaps; razors will be concaved and honed to order in a most satisfactory manner. Violins and strings as well as violin fixtures of all kinds, and watches, jewelry, etc., are constantly carried in stock, and sold at retail. Mr. Amazeen employs two competent assistants, and gives close personal attention to all departments of his business, and being thoroughly acquainted with every detail of the business, he is very popular with his customers, as his experience and good taste enables him to render valuable assistance when it is desired. A variety of goods is offered, and includes the very latest styles. The public will find it to their advantage to patronize this establishment when they desire anything in the above-named lines of goods. Mr. Amazeen assumed entire control of the business in 1872, since which date he has acquired the reputation of being one of the most enterprising men in Houlton and vicinity.

L. T. CLOUGH, Livery, Boarding and Exchange Stable. Good Horses and a Driver, when required. Carrying Lumbermen a specialty. Mechanic Street, Houlton, Me.—Mr. Clough carries on one of the most widely popular stables in this section, and no one can do business with him for any length of time without conceding that the popularity referred to, is by no means the result of luck or chance, but on the contrary, is the legitimate result of straightforward methods and an evident desire to treat every customer fairly and liberally. He is a native of Maine and has conducted this business since 1885 which has steadily increased from the commencement. He is prepared to furnish good horses with a driver whenever required, and teams of a character that makes them presentable everywhere, at short notice and at reasonable rates. He has excellent facilities for boarding horses, having about thirty stalls. The owners of horses that are boarded here, feel assured that they have comfortable quarters as well as the best of food and care. An important department of Mr. Clough's business is the buying, selling and exchanging of horses, and as his stable is so well known to the purchasing public, he is able to dispose of many animals to good advantage. Employment is given to competent help that customers may be promptly and satisfactorily served.

CHARLES P. TENNEY, Dry Goods, Boots, Shoes, Hats, Caps and Gents' Furnishing Goods, 58 Main Street, Houlton, Me.—The popularity of the establishment conducted by Mr. Charles P. Tenney is by no means the result of luck, but on the contrary, has been brought about by hard, intelligent and faithful work continued through nearly a half century of years. The proprietor is a native of Houlton, and became identified with his present enterprise about 1851. He deals in dry goods, boots, shoes, hats, caps and gents' furnishing goods. The premises occupied are located at No. 58 Main street, comprising two floors and a basement each of the dimensions of 22x80 feet, affording space for the accommodation of quite an extensive stock, and on the score of magnitude alone Mr. Tenney's assortment is paralleled by few if any similar stocks in this section, but its quality is even more remarkable than its quantity, and the very latest fashionable novelties are always well represented. All classes of trade are catered to and the closest buyers agree that at no store in this section is more genuine value given for money received. Four reliable and well informed assistants are employed. Callers are assured prompt and courteous attention, goods being cheerfully shown and every opportunity given to make a deliberate and satisfactory selection.

E. B. WHITE, dealer in Watches, Clocks and Jewelry, Spectacles, Guns, Ammunition, Fishing Tackle, etc., etc. Fine Watch Repairing a specialty. No. 5½ Market Square, Houlton, Me.— One of the most reliable and attractive establishments in this vicinity is that conducted by Mr. E. B. White, who is a dealer in watches, clocks, jewelry, spectacles, guns, ammunition, fishing tackle, etc. His stock is of course bright and handsome but still it owes a good part of its attractive qualities to the taste and skill with which it is arranged. Business was commenced here in 1884, and the public have long since learned that the articles bought at this store are sure to prove just as they are represented in every respect. Mr. White offers a fine line of watches and clocks and he quotes the lowest market prices for them. Every person should have a good time-keeper and the opportunity for procuring one for a little money was never better than now. A well selected stock of jewelry is kept on hand and particular attention is called to the novelties offered in this department. He also carries an excellent collection of sportsman's articles which cannot fail to give satisfaction to those using them. His goods are all reliable and are of the best quality. Mr. White makes a specialty of fine watch repairing, and those who have patronized him in this department can testify to the superior manner in which the work was performed. He is a native of Hope, Me.

E. MERRITT & SONS, Millers and wholesale dealers in Potatoes, Hay, Grain and Short Lumber; Proprietors Houlton Flour and Plaster Mills and Houlton Incandescent Light, Houlton, Me.—The business carried on under the firm-name of E. Merritt & Sons was founded more than a quarter of a century ago, in 1865, and has long ranked among those representative enterprises which combine to make Houlton the trade centre for all the country adjacent. The senior partner died in 1885, and the undertaking is now carried on by Messrs. C. D. and L. B. Merritt, both of whom are natives of Massachusetts. Mr. C D. Merritt has served as county treasurer and is now town treasurer, and both members of the firm are so widely known in business and social circles that extended personal mention is quite unnecessary. The concern are millers, and wholesale dealers in potatoes, hay, grain and short lumber, and are proprietors of the Houlton Flour and Plaster Mills and the Houlton Incandescent Light; they operating the electric lighting plant by which the town is illuminated. Their store is 28×120 feet in dimensions, and contains a heavy stock of grain, flour, etc. A well stocked meat and provision market is also conducted by this firm, everything being of uniformly dependable quality and offered at prices in strict accordance with the lowest market rates. The firm do a very large wholesale business in potatoes, hay and grain, shingles and other short lumber, and are prepared to fill the very heaviest orders at short notice and to quote bottom prices on all the commodities handled; their facilities being unsurpassed.

H. J. HATHEWAY, wholesale and retail dealer in Drugs, Medicines and Chemicals, Fancy and Toilet Articles, Sponges, Brushes, Perfumery, etc.; sole agent for the Standard Liniment; Houlton, Me.—We are sure there are no residents of Houlton but what are acquainted with the enterprise conducted by Mr. H. J. Hatheway, who is a wholesale and retail dealer in drugs, medicines and chemicals. There is no similar establishment in this vicinity that is more popular or more worthy of popularity. This business was started in 1872 by Page & Cary, but in 1873 they were succeeded by the present proprietor. He has thus carried on this business for about eighteen years, and he has succeeded in winning the confidence of this community by keeping his assortment of goods so full and complete, as to be able to meet all

demands that may be made upon it. Callers at this store are received with uniform courtesy and served with care and promptness. The usual line of druggist's sundries are handled, including fancy and toilet articles, sponges, brushes, perfumery, etc. The premises occupied contain about 1600 feet of space. Only the purest ingredients are sold and every effort is used to give complete satisfaction to all. Two efficient assistants are employed. Mr. Hatheway manufactures the Standard Liniment, also Jackson's cough syrup, Rose hair wash and Sarsaparilla. He is a native of Eastport, Me., and served in the army during our late Rebellion.

J. J. ROYAL, Manufacturer and Dealer in Harnesses and Horse Clothing, Carriage Robes, Whips, etc., Houlton, Me.—The difference between "goods cheap" and "cheap goods" is apt to be forgotten by those who are economically disposed, but it is well worthy of being carefully borne in mind, especially when anything in the line of harness or horse furnishings is to be bought. The common "cheap" harness is but a miserable makeshift at the best, to say nothing of the danger of using a harness that is liable to give way the moment any unusual strain is brought upon it. Considerations of economy alone should prevent its being bought, for it has no durability, and must constantly be "patched up" in one way or another Mr. J. J. Royal, is a maker of and dealer in harnesses, and he can give intending purchasers no better advice than to give him a call, for, although his productions are honestly and skillfully made from selected stock, they are offered at low rates, quality and durability being of course duly considered. Mr. Royal is a native of Hodgdon, Me., and has carried on his present undertaking here in Houlton since 1880. He is a manufacturer, as well as dealer in harnesses and horse clothing, and is agent for Vitae Lotion, the celebrated veterinary liniment. Sewing machines will be repaired in a thoroughly workmanlike manner at short notice, while needles and repairs for all kinds of sewing machines are carried in stock. Mr. Royal offers a full assortment of horse goods at bottom prices, embracing late novelties in this line, as well as all the staple goods A carefully chosen stock of harnesses, horse clothing, carriage robes, etc., are always on hand to select from, every article being sold under a guarantee that it will prove as represented.

ESTABLISHED 1889.

WILLIAM H. SMITH

✴ PRINTER ✴

68 MAIN ST.,   HOULTON, ME.

I especially invite the patronage of those who desire their work well done. Special estimates given on large orders, and prompt and careful attention to every order, whatever the quantity.

FINE BOOK AND COMMERCIAL PRINTING
A SPECIALTY.

Prices Reasonable for First-class Work.

"Nothing conveys so poor an impression of a business house as cheap and poorly printed office stationery."

HOULTON SAVINGS BANK, Houlton, Me. —Young men and young women are given a great deal of advice nowadays, but there is one bit of advice which is often forgotten and more often not followed when given, and that is—save money. And yet to those who have their own way to make in the world no more valuable advice can be given, and those who follow it may be trusted to take care of themselves under all ordinary and some extraordinary circumstances, for one who practices the habit of money saving has learned to depend upon himself, to some extent, at least. He is almost sure to be industrious, is not at all apt to indulge freely in intoxicating liquors, is pretty sure to take every opportunity to better his condition, and in short is one who not only deserves success but may be depended upon to win it. The habit is by no means difficult to acquire. A little self-denial and prudence will enable practically any young man to save something every week or every month, and the task soon becomes easy, for a good habit is as binding as a bad one, and a self-made men agree that the first $500 or $1,000 they accumulated was the hardest to get together, not only because it was then they were forming the habit of saving, but also because "money makes money," and a small capital well managed will rapidly increase. Begin at once and put by something every pay-day, even if you can save only a little at first; the great thing is to get the habit of putting *at least* a certain amount aside, and when this is done the rest will be easy. Of course you should deposit in a well-managed savings bank, and you may search the State and not find a better managed one than the Houlton Savings Bank, as is proved by its record since its organization in 1872. This institution now has more than a quarter of a million of dollars confided to it, the amount due depositors May 1, 1891 having been $294,631.62, and it then had a surplus above all liabilities of $8,368.55, as computed by the bank examiner, Mr. George D. Bisbee. But favorable as this showing is, it is not so conclusive of the unsurpassed standing of the

bank as is the character of the men identified with its management, as our readers will agree after an examination the annexed list of officers and trustees : President, Almon H. Fogg ; vice-president, Frederick A. Powers ; treasurer, L. O. Ludwig ; trustees, Silas T. Plummer, Don A. H. Powers, O. F. French, Thomas M. Bradbury, Samuel Lane, Simon Friedman, George H. Freeman, Black Hawk Putnam, J. H. Bradford, Charles D. Merritt.

THE FIRST NATIONAL BANK, Houlton, Me.—The First National Bank of Houlton was incorporated in 1881, but did not commence business until August 1, 1882, so that it has been in operation just about nine years—long enough certainly to enable an intelligent judgment of its policy to be formed by a study of its past record, present condition and future prospects. A judgment so formed by a competent and unprejudiced observer will surely be favorable in the case of this bank, for its affairs have been and are ably administered, and it has unquestionably done much to advance the interests of this town and this section of the State by furnishing first class financial facilities, and adhering closely to the fundamental principles governing truly legitimate banking. The temptation to depart from those principles under the exigencies of the close competition which is present in banking no less than in other business in these modern times, is sometimes great—how great is indicated by the many cases in which such departure has been followed by embarrassment and sometimes ruin—but the management of this representative institution have steadily resisted all speculative tendencies and based their action on the solid rock of absolutely unimpaired credit, recognizing that to maintain that was and is their chief duty to depositors and the general public no less than to the bank itself. As a natural, and, indeed, inevitable consequence, the First National Bank of Houlton enjoys the fullest confidence of the community in general and the business public in particular, and affords a service unsurpassed for reliability and efficiency by that of any other financial institution in the State. Particular attention is paid to collections, and all the services incidental to a regular banking business will be rendered on as liberal terms as are consistent with careful regard for the interests of all parties concerned. The officers and directors are far too generally known to need personal introduction to our readers, as will be seen by an examination of the following list : Walter Mansur, president ; Charles P. Tenney, vice-president ; William C. Donnell, cashier ; directors, Walter Mansur, Charles P. Tenney, Clarence H. Pierce, James Frank Holland, Hudson T. Frisbie, William H. Gray, Almon H. Fogg.

J. R. LOWE, Lumber, Moulding and Planing Mill, Houlton, Me.—The great and growing popularity of hard wood flooring is due in a measure, of course, to the fact that the public appreciate more fully than formerly that hard-wood floors are the cleanest and most healthful, besides being the cheapest in the long run, as they may be left bare or be covered by rugs that will wear a great deal longer than carpets, but it is also due to reduction in the cost of hard wood flooring made possible by the use of improved machinery. A visit to the mill carried on by Mr. J. R. Lowe will show that he is prepared to furnish hard wood flooring in quantities to suit as cheap as anybody else, for he makes a specialty of its manufacture and having first class facilities is in a position to meet all honorable competition. The mill is two stories in height and 40×60 feet in dimensions, and there is a spacious dry-house connected. The machinery is of the most improved type and power is furnished by a forty-horse engine ; employment being given to from five to eight assistants and orders being promptly and accurately filled. Besides making hard wood flooring Mr. Lowe manufactures builders' finish of all kinds, and does matching, planing and sawing to order at short notice and at uniformly reasonable rates.

F. R. SMITH.   A. P. SMITH.

SMITH BROTHERS,

MANUFACTURERS OF AND DEALERS IN

STOVES AND TINWARE,

SHEET LEAD AND LEAD PIPE.

Agents for the Atlantic Wood Furnace. Plumbing and Piping a Specialty.

Market Square,   -   -   Houlton, Maine.

G. W. RICHARDS & CO., dealers in Dry and Fancy Goods, Domestic Hand-Knit Socks, Mitts and Drawers Bought and Sold, Houlton, Me.—Operations were commenced in this line of trade by Messrs. Page & Stevens, who was succeeded by A. B. Page. He was succeeded by Mr. F. C. Nickerson and it was in 1886 when the present proprietors Mr. G. W. Richards & Co., took possession of these premises which are about 25×95 feet in dimensions. To say that this store has become more popular and more largely patronized than many other stores in this town, is merely to assert what every resident of Houlton knows to be a fact, for Messrs. Richards & Co., have such an accurate idea of what the public want and have shown such an enterprise in catering to all classes of patrons, that their establishment has become a favorite resort of those seeking the latest novelties in dry and fancy goods. The stock on hand comprise a full line of dry and fancy goods which are offered at a very moderate price, as Richards & Co., are careful buyers and believe in sharing the advantages so gained with their customers. They have also a variety of domestic hand-knit socks, mitts and drawers, which they are prepared to sell to the advantage of those using such articles, and which they are willing to purchase if of a superior make and finish. Employment is given to four assistants, and as the firm are thoroughly familiar with every detail of their business, they are well informed as to the latest novelties in the New York and Boston markets, and spare no pains to keep their stock fully "up to the times" in every respect. This firm was the first to adopt the "Cash Railway" system in Aroostook Co.

W. G. SOMERVILLE, Meat and Groceries, Houlton, Me.—Among those establishments which both on account of the character and extent of the stock carried and the low prices named on the articles comprising the same, are worthy of especially prominent and favorable mention, must be classed that conducted by Mr. W. G. Somerville, for this gentleman caters to the most fastidious trade, while his prices are as low as the lowest in every department, quality of course being considered. The premises are of spacious dimensions and afford ample accommodation for the heavy assortment of fresh meats, choice staple and fancy groceries which are constantly carried. A full selection of everything usually carried in a first-class meat and grocery store is always to be found here. Employment is given to thoroughly competent and experienced assistants, all orders being promptly and courteously filled at all times. This establishment was originally founded by Mr. H. C. Arnold, who was succeeded in 1888 by Charles Wilson, and he in 1889 by the firm of Somerville Bros., the present proprietor, Mr. W. G. Somerville assuming full control of the business in 1869. He gives the details of his business careful personal supervision and spares no pains to assure complete satisfaction to the most critical customers.

DR. H. A. GREENE, Dental Surgeon, Houlton, Me.—Pain has been defined as "the prayer of the nerve for relief," and if we accept this definition, we must confess that some nerves, and especially those connected with the teeth, have a style of praying which is much more forcible than enjoyable. Nature, of course, has some good reason for making the nerves of the teeth so sensitive, and, indeed, even under present conditions, many of us neglect our teeth in a most shameful manner. When once they are put in good order it is not difficult to keep them so, and as the services of a competent dentist are indispensable, if this result is to be attained, we take pleasure in calling the attention of our readers to the facilities offered by Dr. H. A. Greene, for he is not only a skilful but a gentle operator, and has the most improved apparatus and instruments to enable him to practice dentistry in all its branches. Dr. Greene began the practice of his profession in 1885, and has been located in Houlton since 1890. He is fast building up an enviable reputation as a well informed and reliable practitioner, and we have no hesitation in guaranteeing satisfaction to those availing themselves of his services, for his methods are thorough but gentle. His work will compare favorably with any with which we are acquainted, and his charges are uniformly moderate. Dr. Greene's office is centrally located over A. H. Fogg & Co.'s store, and all callers may depend upon receiving prompt and careful attention.

H. O. BERRY, Carriage Making, Repairing, Painting, Houlton, Me.—The chances are that a great many owners and users of carriages and wagons are included among our readers, and the establishment carried on by Mr. H. O. Berry, at Houlton, is of especial interest to this class, for Mr. Berry is a carriage manufacturer as well as repairer and painter. He has the most improved facilities at hand for the manufacture of heavy team wagons, and the repairing and painting of all kinds of vehicles. Mr. Berry is a native of Smyrna, Me., and has been identified with his present enterprise since 1875. The premises made use of include two floors each 25×60 feet in dimensions and are completely fitted up for the requirements of the work done. Employment being given to experienced assistants, so that orders can be filled at short notice—a point that will be especially appreciated by those who want a carriage or a wagon repaired, and cannot afford to be long deprived of the use of it. The work done here is dependable in the full sense of the word, for selected material is used, and the workmanship is first class throughout. Everything considered, the prices quoted by Mr. Berry will compare very favorably with those named elsewhere, and it is well to bear in mind that he warrants his work in every particular. Therefore those who find it difficult to get their work done promptly and in a satisfactory manner would do well to make Mr. Berry a call.

RICKER CLASSICAL INSTITUTE,

HOULTON, MAINE.

Beautifully Located,
Fine Buildings,
Broad Curriculum,
High Moral Tone.

This school now ranks among the first in the State. There are four courses of study, College Preparatory, Academic, Normal and English.

A dormitory is connected with the school where students may obtain board or rooms at a low price.

TUITION:—English branches at the rate of fifty cents per week ; Languages at the rate of sixty cents per week.

Further information as to terms, etc., freely supplied to any one who will write to the principal,

ARTHUR M. THOMAS.

AROOSTOOK HOMESPUN YARNS, manufactured by W. H. Esty, Houlton, Me.—There has been a woolen mill in Houlton for many years, and it is safe to say that no other mill in the country has been carried on on more straightforward principles, or turned out goods that were more dependable in every respect. The proprietor, Mr. W. H. Esty, fully maintains the reputation of the establishment, and it is known throughout this section that anything coming from these mills represents, as "all wool," is precisely that and nothing else, being therefore radically different from the greater part of the "all wool" goods now so common in the market. This is a one set mill and produces the famous "Aroostook" hom spun yarns, all-wool flannels, woolen suitings, satinets, bed blankets and horse blankets. These goods are sold at both wholesale and retail, and the prices named on them are always moderate and in some cases exceptionally low. There is a carpet cleaning machine connected with the mill, and carpets will be *thoroughly* cleaned without injury, and at very short notice, the rates being low enough to suit the most economically disposed.

ALMON H. FOGG & CO., jobbers and retailers of Hardware, Cutlery, Paints and Oils, House Trimmings and Farming Tools, 72 to 78 Main Street, Houlton, Me.—The enterprise conducted by Messrs. Almon H. Fogg & Co. was established more than thirty years ago and has borne a very prominent part in the work of bringing about the present importance of Houlton as a business centre. It was founded in 1859 and has steadily developed until it has reached very large proportions, the business comprising many departments each of which is most efficiently conducted, the result being that both wholesale and retail buyers of hardware, cutlery, farming tools, paints and oils, glass, house trimmings, etc., are assured unsurpassed value for money paid and the prompt and accurate filling of their orders by taking advantage of the facilities offered by this representative firm, composed of Messrs. Almon H. Fogg and Clarence H. Pierce, the former a native of Bangor, and the latter of Houlton. Mr. Fogg has served as Town Treasurer, and has been president of the Houlton Savings Bank since its organization in 1872. The concern carry an immense stock and utilize very spacious premises, including four floors measuring about 60×70 feet, and a two-story storehouse of the dimensions of 125×30 feet. Employment is given to six assistants, and notwithstanding the magnitude of the business, immediate and careful attention is assured to every caller.

O. NEWHOUSE, Groceries and Provisions, Dry Goods, and Boots and Shoes, Houlton, Me.—The business now carried on by Mr. O. Newhouse at Houlton, Me., was founded by him in 1875. Mr. Newhouse is a native of Germany and has been in business in the States for thirty four years, and is therefore thoroughly familiar with the practical details of his present line of trade, giving the business careful personal supervision and raising the service to the highest standard of efficiency. Mr. Newhouse is a dealer in general merchandise and utilizes commodious premises, comprising one floor and basement, each 25×60 feet in dimensions, a large stock is carried, among the more important commodities handled being choice staple and fancy groceries, provisions, dry goods, and boots and shoes. These are selected especially with a view to supplying regular trade, and hence may be depended upon to prove entirely satisfactory as they come from the most reliable sources and are in every instance guaranteed to prove just as represented. Mr. Newhouse believes in "quick sales and small profits," and quotes bottom prices on everything he handles. Competent and reliable assistants are employed and immediate and careful attention is thus assured to every caller. Mr. Newhouse also deals extensively in raw furs and pays the highest price.

SILAS W. TABER, manufacturer of Fine Carriages, Sleighs, etc., etc. ; Jobbing of all kinds promptly attended to ; ordered work a specialty ; Mechanic Street, Houlton, Me.—Mr. Taber is one of the best known manufacturers of fine carriages, sleighs, etc., in this neighborhood. He commenced operations about twenty-seven years ago, and his business has continued to increase from the start. Those of our readers who wish to procure a fine carriage or sleigh can do no better than to give an order for the same to Mr. Silas W. Taber, for he makes a specialty of such work and can guarantee perfect satisfaction as to quality, style and price. He is also prepared to attend to jobbing of all kinds, which is promptly attended to. All work entrusted to him may be safely depended upon to prove just as represented, the practice of covering up defective work with handsome paint not being allowed at this establishment. The premises are located on Mechanic street, Houlton, Me., and they have all facilities for producing good work. Employment is given to eight competent men, that every order may be filled when promised. Mr. Taber is a native of this town, and is well and favorably known in all adjacent towns.

O. F. FRENCH,

Main and Court Streets, Houlton, Maine,

DEALER IN

DRUGS, MEDICINES AND CHEMICALS,

FANCY AND TOILET ARTICLES,

SPONGES, BRUSHES, PERFUMERY, ETC.

PHYSICIANS' PRESCRIPTIONS CAREFULLY COMPOUNDED.

A. P. M. TABER, Horse Shoer and Farrier ; Regulating Horses Teeth a specialty ; agent for Glaisier's Peat Moss Petroleum ; Houlton, Me.—Mr. Taber, who is a native of Houlton, Me., has conducted this business for about twenty years and we believe now takes the lead in his especial line. A blacksmith's shop is as necessary in a community as almost any line of business which can be mentioned, but in order to be ranked among the leading places, it must be first class in every respect, and any one wishing a strictly first class job done at a moderate price should visit this shop. Mr. Taber makes a specialty of shoeing horses and treating and regulating their teeth. He is also competent to treat them for other ailments. Those who own valuable horses can appreciate the services of one who understands their diseases and the great advantage of having so skillful a person in town, and there are many gentlemen in this neighborhood who have availed themselves of this great convenience. Mr. Taber is agent for Peat Moss medicated hoof stuffing.

I. M. HILL & CO., successors to John M. Rice, Furniture, Carpets, etc. ; Undertaking a specialty ; West End Public Square, Houlton, Me.—It is certainly not to be wondered at that Messrs. I. M. Hill & Co. should do a very large and constantly growing business, for the advantages gained by dealing with them are so many and obvious that there is little chance of even the most careless buyer failing to appreciate them. To begin with, they occupy very extensive premises which consist of four floors, each about 1500 feet in dimensions. These afford excellent facilities for the display and examination of the goods to be sold, which includes furniture, carpets, etc. His stock is a very valuable and desirable one and it is complete in its variety and style. The furniture is thoroughly made and the designs are new. The carpets represent some of the newest patterns of the best houses, while the prices for the same are very moderate. Messrs. Hill & Co. make a specialty of undertaking, and they are prepared to assume entire charge of funerals, and to supply every thing required for such occasions at very reasonable rates. Mr. John M. Rice conducted this business for more than fifteen years, and it was in 1889 that the present firm of I. M. Hill & Co. succeeded him. Mr. Hill is a native of Littleton, Me. The firm enjoy the fullest confidence of the public as their goods are never knowingly misrepresented and their prices are always low as the lowest.

D. F. CHAMPEON, Electrician ; orders for Electrical Apparatus promptly attended to ; Electrical Repair Work solicited ; Agents for the "Acme" Cash Railway System ; 23 Court Street, Houlton, Me.—In order that electrical apparatus should give satisfaction it is essential that it be properly arranged and connected, and, obvious as this fact would seem to be, it is apparently often lost sight of, for many persons seem to believe that as long as they obtain first-class apparatus it will surely work well whether they or other unskilled persons put it up, the consequence being that the work is improperly done, the apparatus fails when most needed, perhaps, and is condemned as "a fraud" or "not practical." This is annoying, to say the least, and it is also wholly unnecessary, for, by placing orders with Mr. D. F. Champeon at No. 23 Court street, satisfactory results are positively assured. He is a native of Exeter, Me. ; began operations in Houlton as a member of the firm of Champeon & Young in 1889, and assumed sole control in 1891. Being an expert practical electrician he is prepared to do all kinds of electrical work, such as putting in electric bells, annunciators, burglar alarms, electric locks, etc., which may be operated from any part of the premises, and to do electrical repair work of every description at short notice, at moderate rates and in the most efficient manner. Mr. Champeon deals in all kinds of electrical apparatus and supplies and will furnish the same at lowest market rates. Speaking tubes and whistles are also dealt in, and gun and locksmithing and bell hanging will be done in first class style at low rates. Electro plating in gold, silver and nickel is also firmly done at this establishment. Mr. Champeon is the sole agent for Maine for the Acme Cash Railway System, which saves time, labor and money, is ornamental as well as useful, and will be rented or sold outright at moderate rates. Mail orders are assured prompt attention, and we feel fully justified in guaranteeing satisfaction to all who may take advantage of Mr. Champeon's facilities.

HENRY B. ESMOND, M. D.,

HOMEOPATHIC PHYSICIAN AND SURGEON,

Office in Putnam and Mansur's Block,   No. 3 Market Square, Houlton, Maine.

CHRONIC AND DIFFICULT CASES SUCCESSFULLY TREATED.

Special Attention given to the Treatment of Diseases of Women and Children.

Medical Examiner for The Union Mutual Life Insurance Company, of Portland, Maine.

L. C. BRYANT, Importer, wholesale and retail dealer in Five, Ten and Twenty-five-Cent Goods; Crockery, Glass and Tin Ware a specialty; Houlton, Me.—So great a variety of articles is included under the head of five, ten and twenty five cent goods that it is quite impossible within our limited space to give anything like a detailed description of the stock carried by Mr. L. C. Bryant, for he is an importer of and a wholesale and retail dealer in such goods, and offers as complete and desirable an assortment as can be found in this section of the State. Mr. Bryant is a native of Machias, and founded his present business in 1884, since which date he has built up a large and still steadily increasing trade by dealing fairly with his patrons and sparing no pains to fully satisfy every reasonable customer. Mr. Bryant occupies one floor and a basement, each measuring 30×40 feet, and has his stock so arranged that inspection of the many articles it comprises is easy and pleasant. A specialty is made of crockery, glass and tin ware, and not only are the latest novelties offered as well as all the staple styles, but the prices quoted average much lower than are generally named on goods of equal merit. Mr. Bryant has recently bought from the well-known firm of E. Merritt & Sons their entire line of crockery and glass ware, and leased their store in the brick block for a term of years, where he is better prepared to handle his large and steadily increasing trade.

JOHN A. MILLAR, Wholesale Grocer and manufacturer of Pure Confectionery; Nos. 9 and 11 Court Street, Houlton, Me.—There is no denying that there has sprung up of late years a certain prejudice against what are known as "grocers' candies," owing to the fact that some grocery houses in their eagerness to overcome all competition in the confectionery line by quoting low prices have supplied their customers with very inferior goods. Only comparatively few houses have done this, but the high-priced confectioners have taken advantage of the opportunity to build up a popular prejudice against "grocers' candies" in general. Now, of course, this is unjust, for many grocers handle only first class confectionery, even if they do undersell the "regular" confectioners, and very prominent among those who quote bottom prices on confectionery of guaranteed excellence is Mr. John A. Millar, doing business at Nos. 9 and 11 Court street. Mr. Millar is a native of New Brunswick, and has carried on his present business since 1879. He is not only a wholesale and retail grocer but also a manufacturer, wholesaler and retailer of pure confectionery, and hence knows just what he is furnishing to his customers in the way of candy, and fully guarantees its purity, while quoting bottom prices on each of the many varieties dealt in. The premises made use of comprise three floors and a basement, measuring 25×65 feet, and are fitted up with all facilities necessary to enable operations to be carried on to the best advantage, the most extensive orders being filled at short notice, as employment is given to eight competent assistants.

JOHN BRYSON, Photographer; Pictures copied and enlarged; Houlton, Me.—Since the time that the great French artist discovered the art of daguerreotyping, photography has been making rapid and continual advances until to-day it occupies a position of commanding influence. The photographic studio now conducted by Mr. John Bryson has been under his management for about thirty years. The popularity and success which he has attained in this business speak most conclusively for his skill as an artist, and the good taste of the people of Houlton. He occupies a fine studio, where he is prepared to offer his patrons the most satisfactory work in all branches of fine photography. Pictures are copied and enlarged in the most approved styles. An examination of his work, and the testimony of his large circle of patrons, will confirm all he claims for his talents and workmanship. He has every modern improvement connected with his business and is prepared to take orders for all kinds and sizes of pictures that come under the head of photography. Mr. Bryson gives employment to three assistants who are competent to perform the duties he requires of them. He is a native of New Brunswick, and he has made many friends in our midst by his courtesy and skill as an artist. Mr. J. Frank Bryson, the son, who is also a fine artist, and a thoroughly good fellow, has recently been admitted to partnership. For fine photographs or out-door views, we most heartily recommend this firm to our readers.

W. A. NICKERSON, wholesale and retail dealer in Dry and Fancy Goods, Furnishing Goods, Fur Coats, Ladies Wraps, Boots, Shoes and Rubbers, 63 Main Street, Houlton, Me.—Notwithstanding the high average character of the many mercantile establishments located in Houlton and vicinity, it is obvious that here, as elsewhere, there must be certain houses in each line of trade which excel all others in the handling of given specialties, and it is an open secret that at the establishment conducted by Mr. W. A. Nickerson at No. 63 Main street, unequaled inducements are offered to purchasers of dry and fancy goods of all kinds, also furnishing goods, fur coats, ladies' wraps, boots, shoes, rubbers, etc. Mr. Nickerson ought to be able to offer exceptional advantages to buyers of these goods, for he has had long and varied experience in his present line of business, and has been located in Houlton since about 1882, and enjoys such favorable relations with producers as to enable him to quote positively bottom prices on positively dependable goods. He is a native of Hodgdon, Me., and has long ranked among Houlton's representative merchants. The premises occupied measure 35×90 feet in dimensions, opportunity being given for the carrying of a very heavy and varied stock, and for the display of it to excellent advantage. Dry and fancy goods, etc., are dealt in both at wholesale and retail, and the employment of five competent assistants assures prompt and polite attention to every customer. Mr. Nickerson is well known throughout Houlton and vicinity, and now holds the office of county treasurer.

C. H. FOWLER,

DEALER IN

Watches, Clocks and Jewelry,

Particular attention given to Fine Watch and Jewelry Repairing.

COURT ST.,   HOULTON, ME.

J. E. BURNHAM, Oyster House, Cigars and Tobacco, Houlton, Me.—The man who carries on an establishment and furnishes food that is all right both as regards quality and quantity is a benefactor to the human race and deserves every credit, and as Mr. J. E. Burnham is just that kind of an individual we take pleasure in commending his establishment to the favorable attention of our readers. The Oyster House under consideration has been under the management of the present proprietor since 1887. He has renovated the premises until they are, among the best in Houlton, and cover an area of some 720 square feet. Mr. Burnham has always been famous for combining good food and plenty of it with low prices, and with his thorough knowledge of the business, he understands the wants of each customer, and always strives to please them. Mr. Burnham is a native of Lincoln, Me., and is very well known throughout Houlton, where he has built up an extensive wholesale and retail business. He deals extensively in oysters, and also carries constantly in stock a choice assortment of cigars, tobacco, etc. The many improvements which Mr. Burnham has made in his business methods should, and we feel assured does assist, in adding much patronage to his establishment.

EXCELSIOR NEWS DEPOT, O. M. Smith, dealer in Books, Stationery, Fancy Goods, Room Paper and Curtains, Jewelry, Musical Merchandise, Sporting Goods, etc., Houlton, Me.—An enterprise of special interest to the people of Houlton, and one that will be of value to learn something about in this volume, is the Excelsior News Depot, conducted by Mr. O. M. Smith. He has been identified with this establishment from the time it was started by the firm of Smith & Lunt in 1885 and since 1889, has had the entire management of affairs. The business of this house is steadily increasing, and its resources are ample to meet all demands. Its policy is worthy the consideration of the public, who will find many advantages in dealing here. Mr. Smith has in his employ two competent assistants, and customers are assured immediate and courteous attention, and that all inquiries will be answered politely. The premises are centrally located and are 24×50 feet in dimensions, and contain not only a choice assortment of books, stationery, and fancy goods, but a large variety of room paper and curtains, also jewelry, musical merchandise and sporting goods, etc. Mr. Smith who is a native of Maine is a man thoroughly conversant with the minutest details concerning the business, to which he gives his close supervision, and our citizens are sure that they can obtain here the most popular publications of the day, as well as the latest novelties in all departments of the establishment. We can therefore commend the able and efficient management of this house.

G. W. LANE, dealer in Boots, Shoes and Rubbers, 17 Court Street, Houlton, Me.—When buying boots or shoes, the main point is to get a pair that will fit you, and it is worth while to take more pains to do this than one would suppose, for not only is good fitting footwear decidedly more comfortable than that which is too loose or too tight at one point or another, but it is also decidedly more durable, as has been repeatedly proved by actual test. Now, feet vary considerably in size and proportions, and hence, the only way to get something that will really fit is to choose from a stock containing practically all sizes and widths, and if you make your selections from the assortment offered by the Boston Shoe Store, Mr. G. W. Lane, proprietor, at No. 17 Court street, you will have little trouble in getting a satisfactory fit, for the stock is exceptionally complete, both as regards sizes and varieties of footwear. Mr. Lane is a young man, and is a native of Boston, where he was connected with the wholesale shoe house of Batchelder & Lincoln for seven years, and it is needless to add, thoroughly understands the business. He began business in Houlton in 1890, and conducts the only exclusive shoe store in this county, including a branch store at Caribou. Mr. Lane spares no pains to keep his assortment of boots, shoes and rubbers complete in every department, and there is practically nothing in the line of seasonable footwear he is not prepared to furnish. His prices are low as the lowest, and as his goods are in every instance guaranteed to prove as represented, no better place to trade can be found in this town.

C. H. WILSON, dealer in Groceries, Provisions, Tobaccos, Fruit and Confectionery, Houlton, Me.—This establishment has been conducted here for many years as Mr. C. H. Wilson succeeded Carey Bros , in 1865, and the grocery trade had been carried on for some years previous to that date. Its present proprietor, Mr. Wilson, ranks among the most important and representative business men, and the service was never more prompt, accurate and generally satisfactory than it is now. The stock on hand is varied and complete, being carefully selected for family use. Choice groceries, provisions, tobaccos, fruit and confectionery are largely dealt in, and despite the uniformly excellent quality of these articles the prices quoted will bear the closest comparison with those of other dealers. Employment is given to three competent assistants, and customers are assured prompt and polite treatment, while orders are accurately filled. The premises contain about 600 feet. Mr. C. H. Wilson who is a native of St. Albans, Me , has been the town treasurer and for four years was in partnership with Mr. T. M. Bradbury. He is very widely and favorably known in this vicinity.

JAMES K. OSGOOD, Jeweler and Optician; also Watches, Clocks, Silverware, and rich Fancy Goods; everything usually kept in a First-class Jewelry Store; Fine Watch Repairing a specialty; 59 Main Street, Houlton, Me. Mr. James K. Osgood is a native of Maine, and is very widely and favorably known in Houlton and vicinity, both in business and social circles, he having made many friends by his enterprising and straightforward methods during the twenty years that he has been identified with the present enterprise. He deals in jewelry, clocks, silverware, rich fancy goods, watches, optical goods, etc. The premises occupied by Mr. Osgood are some 600 square feet in dimensions, and located at 59 Main street, Houlton, a very carefully chosen stock of American watches, clocks, jewelry, silverware, engagement and wedding rings being always on hand to choose from, and is so frequently renewed as to always contain many of the latest novelties, besides full lines of staple goods, diamonds, rich jewelry, spectacles, etc., styles which are in permanent demand. The leading makes of Waltham, Elgin, Hampden, Springfield and all makes of standard American watches are well represented, and one may buy a good reliable timekeeper here at very low figures, and have the satisfaction of knowing that it is fully guaranteed to prove as represented. Excellent value is also offered in rich fancy goods, and in fact everything usually kept in a first-class jewelry store. A specialty is made of eye-glasses, spectacles and optical goods suited to all defects of vision are furnished at lowest figures possible for good stock. The best lines of silver and plated ware to be found in the market are in stock here. Fine watch repairing a specialty, and will be done in a superior manner at short notice.

T. M. & J. BRADBURY, dealers in Groceries, Carriages, Harnesses, Robes, etc. ; also carry on first-class Livery, Boarding and Sale Stables; Market Square, Houlton, Me.—Messrs. T. M. & J. Bradbury are among the most favorably, as well as the most widely known of Houlton's business men, for their honorable and enterprising methods cause them to be held in high esteem by those with whom they have dealings, and the nature of their undertaking—or rather undertakings, for they carry on three distinct lines of business—has made them almost universally known in this section of the State. Messrs. T. M. and J. Bradbury are both natives of Maine and began business here in Houlton about fifteen years ago. Their store is located on Market square, and has all necessary facilities for the proper accommodation of a varied stock, comprising groceries of all kinds as well as harnesses, robes, etc. These goods are offered at the lowest market rates and a large retail business is done in both departments, requiring the services of three capable assistants. In addition to the lines of business already mentioned, Messrs. T. M. & J. Bradbury carry on a first-class livery, boarding and sale stable. They also carry a large stock of fine carriages of all descriptions. Their establishment is very conveniently arranged and has every facility for the loarding of horses and care of vehicles at reasonable rates. They keep for livery purposes a large number of stylish turnouts. All animals entrusted to their care, either for sale or to board, will be given the best attention, and everything for their comfort will be provided.

FRED F. FRISBIE, wholesale and retail dealer in Fine Groceries, Opposite Snell House, 21 Market Square, Houlton, Me.—Among the many grocery stores located in Houlton, few are better known than that carried on by Mr. Fred F. Frisbie at No. 21 Market street. He began business in 1880 in the boot and shoe line, but since 1888 has been engaged in the grocery business, and has already made an enviable reputation for reliability and fair dealing. Premises of the dimensions of 20×83 feet are occupied, and three courteous and competent assistants are required to attend to the heavy patronage enjoyed. The stock carried at this establishment will compare favorably in all essential features with that of any similar house in Houlton, for it is both large and varied, and contains no commodities of inferior quality, it being Mr. Frisbie's endeavor to cater to the best trade. He does not do this by placing his prices so high that none but the favored few can afford to trade with him, but offers such inducements that experienced buyers feel they can hardly afford to trade elsewhere. A specialty is made of first-class groceries of all kinds, which are sold at both wholesale and retail. The premises occupied are located at No. 21 Market Square, opposite Snell House, where everything sold is guaranteed to prove just as represented, and the prices as low as the lowest, when the quality is considered. Mr. Frisbie being a native of Houlton, is well known and highly respected throughout this vicinity.

H. T. FRISBIE, dealer in Fine Dry Goods and Carpetings, 25 Market Square, Houlton, Me.—It is not a wonderment that the house whose card we print above should be considered as a representative of its class in this vicinity, for it is controlled by a man who has had an extended and varied experience in the business he conducts, and who spares neither pains nor expense to fully maintain the leading position which he has for some time held. The enterprise in question was inaugurated by Mr. H. T. Frisbie in 1866, and has therefore been under the management of the present proprietor for the past quarter of a century. Mr. Frisbie is a native of Houlton, and is very widely known and highly esteemed in this vicinity. The premises occupied are located at 25 Market square comprising two floors each 30×83 feet in dimensions, where the stock carried is not only heavy but complete and includes fine dry goods, and carpetings of every description. Employment is given to three competent assistants and customers are served with promptness and courtesy. The ladies of Houlton have long since learned that when they wish to inspect the latest fashionable novelties this establishment is the place at which to find them, and also that both dry goods and carpetings, are offered at prices which will bear the strictest comparison with those asked elsewhere. The stock includes all grades, and some decided bargains are sure to be found at this popular establishment.

SNELL HOUSE, J. R. Kimball, Proprietor, Houlton, Me.—There is no question but that the standing of a town, among strangers at least, is largely dependent upon the character of its hotel accommodations, and the excellent reputation of Houlton as a town to do business in, or to visit on a pleasure trip, is due in a great measure to the enterprise and liberality shown in the management of its public houses. The Snell House occupies a prominent position among these establishments, for the pleasantness and convenience of its location, as well as the excellence of the accommodations afforded, which commend it to the favorable attention of the most fastidious traveller. This house has forty sleeping-rooms that are comfortably furnished and conveniently arranged and the house is lighted by electricity. The table is supplied with the best the market affords and the cooking is excellent. The service is prompt and obliging as fourteen capable assistants are employed that there may be no delay in the attendance due to guests. The terms of this house are

very reasonable, both to transient and permanent guests. This house was established sometime since and conducted by Mr. Floyd, who was succeeded by Mr. Philbrick. It was in 1888 that the present proprietor, Mr. J. R. Kimball assumed control, and the patronage he has secured is evidence of his fitness for the position. He is a native of Calais, Me, and successfully conducted the St. Croix Exchange for five years.

GILLIN BROTHERS, wholesale and retail dealers in Meats, Groceries, Provisions, Crockery, Fruit and Confectionery : manufacturers of Full Cream Cheese ; dealers in Hay and Short Lumber ; one door east of Post-Office, Houlton, Me.—A large proportion of our readers can no doubt remember when "Groceries and West India goods," was the regulation sign in front of every well-ordered grocery store, but of late years the number of articles comprised under the general head of "groceries," has become so great that no effort is made to indicate the particular portion of the world from whence they came, the fact being that every climate and about every people are represented in the commodities offered. A visit to such an establishment as that conducted by Gillin Brothers, is sure to prove interesting for here may be found an immense assortment of meats, groceries, provisions, crockery, fruit and confectionery. They are manufacturers of full cream cheese and also dealers in hay and short lumber. This firm do an extensive wholesale and retail business and carry goods suited to all classes of trade. The premises made use of are 21×95 feet in dimensions, thus giving ample opportunity for the accommodation of a very large stock, and it is evident at a glance that this opportunity is fully improved. This enterprise was inaugurated by Williams & Co., who were succeeded in 1883 by the present firm of James and D. H. Gillin, both being natives of Houlton, Me. They are widely and favorably known in business and social circles.

LANE & PEARCE, dealers in Dry and Fancy Goods, Boots, Shoes, School Books and Stationery, Red Store, Houlton, Me.—The business conducted by Messrs. Lane & Pearce, was founded in 1878 by Mr. Samuel Lane and has long been looked upon as one of the most truly representative enterprises of the kind in Houlton. Since passing under the control of the present firm in 1886, it has become more popular than ever, for not only has the old reputation for square dealing been fully maintained but increased pains have been taken to keep the stock complete in every department, to handle none but reliable goods and to quote prices as low as the lowest, while it is generally conceded that at no store of the kind in this vicinity is the service more prompt, courteous and generally efficient. The premises are about 25×100 feet in dimensions and no space is wasted either, for a heavy stock is carried, comprising full lines of dry and fancy goods, boots and shoes, stationery, etc. This establishment is familiarly known as the Red Store to the residents of Houlton. Its proprietors, Messrs. Samuel Lane and Varney Pearce, being natives of Maine, and thoroughly familiar with the handling of the merchandise included in their stock, give close personal attention to the many details of their business. Two competent assistants are employed, and the goods are sold strictly on their merits, every article being fully guaranteed to prove precisely as represented.

JOHN BOYLE, Merchant Tailor, Court Street, Houlton, Me.—This establishment has long been a familiar one to the residents of this town, for it was under way previous to 1862, when it was managed by Mr. Charles McCrystle, who was succeeded in 1869 by the present proprietor, Mr. John Boyle. Those familiar with Mr. Boyle's methods of doing business need not be told that he pays more attention to performance than to promise, and every intelligent man knows that it is not the business firm that makes the most extravagant claims that may be

depended upon to afford the best possible service. The experience of Mr. Boyle as a merchant tailor, and the relations that have been so long continued with producers and wholesalers, enable him to procure his articles on favorable terms and to offer them at as low prices as can be quoted on goods of equal merit. His stock contains a full assortment of woolens and suitings, embracing the new and fashionable styles of the season, which will be made up to order in the best style and at the lowest rate for the quality of the goods and work. Mr. Boyle feels confident of giving satisfaction in every respect, and is pleased to show his goods and to assist with his knowledge in selecting material to the best advantage. Orders will receive prompt attention, employment being given to six assistants, and with the close supervision of Mr. Boyle all tastes can be suited.

HOULTON STEAM LAUNDRY AND DYE HOUSE, M. L. Hutchinson, Proprietor, Houlton, Me.— The enterprise conducted under the name of the Houlton Steam Laundry and Dye House, is rapidly and steadily gaining in popularity and patronage under its present management, and for reasons so obvious that they must be apparent even to the most careless observers. The objections raised against the ordinary public laundries and dye houses, are that the work is sometimes only partially done, the goods are apt to be injured by chemicals or by improper handling, and the delivery is uncertain. None of these apply to the establishment in question, the proprietor of which guarantees perfect satisfaction, and is prepared to carry out that guarantee to the letter. All kinds of work is received, for the establishment is equipped with the most improved machinery, skilled and careful assistants are employed, and in short the facilities at hand, are fully equal to the best. This enterprise was originated by Mr. Charles Holt, who was succeeded by the present proprietor, Mr. M. L. Hutchinson in 1889. The premises occupied comprise two floors which are so admirably arranged as to obviate all confusion, and make any errors in the handling and delivery of work of very rare occurrence. Agencies are maintained at Presque Isle, Caribou, Fort Fairfield and Patten. Mr. Hutchinson gives close personal attention to the business and spares no pains to maintain the service at the very highest standard. Very reasonable rates are quoted in both the laundry and dyeing departments, and those who place a trial order at this establishment are sure to become regular patrons. Mr. Hutchinson also manufactures a very fine grade of wool mats.

J. H. WINGATE, dealer in Boots, Shoes and Gents' Furnishings, 41 Market Square, Houlton, Me.—The most successful buyer is the one who discriminates the most successfully between "goods cheap" and "cheap goods," and it is just such a buyer who will find the most to admire in the assortment of boots, shoes and gents' furnishings offered by Mr. J. H. Wingate at No. 41 Market Square, for this gentleman carries on business on the "quick sales and small profits" system, and both his goods and his prices combine to form a very powerful argument in favor of patronizing his establishment. The residents of Houlton and vicinity are too intelligent not to perceive the force of an argument of this kind, and the natural result is that his store is a popular resort, and is gaining in favor daily. It was originally started by Mr. L. Stevens, who was succeeded by Mr. Harry Jenkins, and he by the firm of Webber & Wingate in 1897, the present proprietor assuming entire control of the business in 1888. Mr. J. H. Wingate is a native of Hallowell, Me and is thoroughly conversant with his business in every detail. He gives personal attention to customers, and employs sufficient assistance to enable him to fill all orders without delay. The premises made use of are 25×60 feet in dimensions, and contain among other things, the largest and most complete line of boots and shoes in town. All feet can be fitted ; all tastes can be suited ; and as for the prices, why, call and see for yourself.

S. H. POWERS, manufacturer and dealer in Furniture, Mattresses, Picture Frames, Caskets, Coffins, Robes, etc.; Warerooms, East of Post office, Main Street, Houlton, Me.—It is undoubtedly true that house furnishing goods are cheaper to-day than they ever were before and that about every man can now furnish his home comfortably and even handsomely, but it is also true that many practically worthless goods are in the market and that the only safe course to take is to place orders with a dealer who has proved himself to be worthy of every confidence. In this connection we may very properly call attention to the establishment conducted by Mr. S. H. Powers, whose warerooms are located on Main street, east of post office, for this gentleman is a manufacturer as well as dealer in furniture, mattresses, picture frames, caskets, coffins, robes, etc., and carries a large and exceptionally complete stock, and during the twenty-six years that he has carried on business he has attained a well deserved reputation for representing things just as they are and for quoting the lowest market rates in every department of his business. Operations were begun by him in 1865 at Houlton, he being formerly engaged in business at Presque Isle, Me. The premises now utilized by Mr. Powers comprise three floors each 24×108 feet in dimensions, the front part of the second floor being used as his residence. Mr. Powers is a native of Blue Hill, Me. He served in the army during our late war, and is highly respected among the enterprising business men of this vicinity. He does an extensive business and constantly carries a complete stock. Orders are acted upon without delay and moderate charges are made under all circumstances.

H. C. BRADBURY, Groceries and Meat, near Depot, Houlton, Me.—The business conducted by Mr. H. C. Bradbury has been carried on just about thirty years, having been founded in 1861 by Messrs. Baker & Bradbury, who were succeeded the same year by Messrs. H. C. and T. M. Bradbury. From 1865 to 1867 Mr. H. C. Bradbury was in the express business, and from 1867 to 1870 was proprietor and manager of a large lumber mill, but in 1870 he resumed connection with the grocery and provision business as a member of the firm of Norcross & Bradbury, assuming sole control the following year, or in 1871, so that for the past score of years he has been sole proprietor. Mr. Bradbury does not give exclusive attention to the handling of groceries and meats, but controls a half-interest in a lumber mill and starch mill at Cary, Me., under the firm-name of Norton & Bradbury, carrying on an extensive commission business in potatoes and lumber. The starch mill is located nine miles from Houlton on the Calais road. His store is located near the Houlton depot and is largely patronized; a large and complete stock of groceries and meats being constantly carried, low prices being quoted and prompt attention given to all, as two competent assistants are employed. Mr. Bradbury is a native of New Limerick, Me., has held the position of county treasurer, and during his long and honorable business career has become one of the best-known merchants and manufacturers in this portion of the State.

C. F. ROSS, Merchant Tailor, Opera House Block, Houlton, Me.—Wonderful improvements have been made in ready-made clothing of late years, without a doubt, but to assert that the very best ready-made garments are as desirable as good custom clothing is as absurd as it would be to try to prove that twice two are five, for it is so obvious as not to require demonstration, that garments made to order are sure to fit better, wear better, and, in short give better satisfaction in every way than those made to fit everybody. That many residents of Houlton and vicinity are convinced of this fact is shown by the liberal patronage accorded Mr. C. F. Ross, and we take pleasure in calling attention to his facilities, for we know that he has both the determination and the ability to thoroughly satisfy every reasonable customer. The business

with which he is identified was founded in 1886 by Mr. H. G. Fuller, and passed under the control of the present owner in 1888. Mr. Ross was born in Houlton, and has had a long and varied experience in fine custom tailoring. He gives personal attention to orders and as he employs twelve assistants, he is in a position to execute commissions at short notice, while his charges are uniformly moderate. The premises occupied are located in Opera House Block, and measure 20×80 feet, affording ample room for the carrying of a complete assortment of foreign and domestic fabrics, comprising the latest fashionable novelties. The leading manufacturers are represented, and the goods are guaranteed to prove precisely what they are, claimed to be in every respect.

M. M. KEATON, manufacturer of Doors, Sash, Mouldings, etc., Planing, Turning, Jig and Band Sawing done to order; North end of Bridge, Houlton, Me.—We speak of a house being "built," nowadays the same we always did, but as a matter of fact, most houses are more "put together," at the present time than they are "built," for both the exterior and the interior fittings are made by machinery, in great factories, and the builder has simply to choose the patterns best suited to his purpose, and see that they are properly arranged and distributed about the structure. Nothing is lost by this practice, and a great deal is gained, for a much better house can be erected for a given sum of money to-day than was ever before the case. One of the best-known manufacturers of doors, sash, mouldings, etc., in this vicinity, is Mr. M. M. Keaton. The business now conducted by him was originally started by Messrs. D. and F. W. Gerow, who were succeeded by the firm of Bradbury & Keaton, the present proprietor assuming entire control of the business in 1876. Mr. M M. Keaton is a native of Houlton and has a very large circle of friends and patrons throughout this vicinity. His mills are located at the north end of bridge, comprising three floors, each measuring 25×60 feet. Every facility is at hand for the manufacture of doors, sash, mouldings. etc.; also for planing, turning, jig and band sawing, which is done to order in the most satisfactory manner. Mr. Keaton does an extensive business, both wholesale and retail in character. He has the reputation of selling reliable goods at bottom figures, and as he is prompt in the delivery of orders at all times, it is not surprising that his establishment should rank with the most popular in this section.

MONAHAN BROS., dealers in Meat, Groceries, Tobacco, Cigars, Fruit, Confectionery and Canned Goods, Houlton, Me.—Although it may seem as if information regarding meat, groceries, etc., was hardly called for, there being so large a number of these establishments to be found throughout every community, still for this very reason we believe that the public will appreciate being told that there may be found a strictly reliable enterprise of this kind, as unfortunately, all of them cannot truthfully be so described. We are confident that those who may favor Messrs. Monahan Brothers with their patronage will have no occasion to regret having done so, for these gentlemen carry on one of the best equipped establishments in Houlton, and propose to do all in their power to fully satisfy their customers. The establishment in question was originally founded by Mr. G. H. Walker, who was succeeded by the present firm in 1887. The premises occupied cover an area of about 3,000 square feet, and a very finely selected stock of meats, groceries, tobacco and cigars, as well as fruits, confectionery and canned goods, is constantly on hand and are supplied at the lowest market rates. The large retail trade transacted by this firm require the services of thoroughly competent assistants. All orders are accurately filled and promptly delivered, perfect satisfaction being guaranteed to every patron. Messrs. E. C. & W. H. Monahan are both natives of New Limerick, Me., and are well known among Houlton's enterprising business men.

HOULTON MARBLE WORKS, H. T. COL-

LINS proprietor; dealer in Monuments, Headstones, Tablets, etc., in Marble and Granite; No. 17 Water Street, Houlton, Me.—Mr. Collins is a manufacturer of and dealer in cemetery work of all descriptions, and is prepared to furnish monuments, headstones, etc., at short notice, and at remarkably low rates. He generally has a fine selection of finished work on hand, including monuments of marble and granite, and has a very extensive assortment of designs which he is prepared to carry out at short notice, and to modify to suit the tastes and means of his customers. It is hardly necessary to say that monumental work must be executed in a first-class manner in order to be at all acceptable, for nothing looks more out of place than cheaply and unskilfully constructed cemetery work. The advantages of using granite for monuments has only been appreciated within the past few years, but as they become better known this material grows rapidly in favor. This stone varies greatly in color and is capable of receiving superior finish and polish. It is often selected above all other stones by those of excellent taste and judgment. Mr. Collins will give personal attention to the taste and desires of customers, and every effort will be made to give satisfaction in regard to the style and price of all work.

FRANK L. COOK, dealer in Books, Station-

ery and Art Goods, Room Papers, Curtains, etc, Picture Framing, Musical Instruments; First National Bank Building, Houlton, Me.—In a book intended for the people, as this is, all information as to how homes may be made beautiful at small expense, cannot fail to be of interest, hence we need offer no apology for calling attention to the fine display of goods made by Mr. Frank L. Cook at his well-known establishment, for there is nothing capable of so thoroughly changing the appearance of a room, or of an entire house, for that matter, as books and art goods. Mr. Cook offers a very skilfully selected assortment to choose from, and whether you wish to purchase a new picture or have an old one re framed, a large and fine variety will be found at the establishment in question, and as the prices are as low as the lowest no one should neglect visiting this store. Books and stationery of all kinds are extensively dealt in, and comprise the latest publication in books, the most novel designs in stationery and art goods, as well as an extensive assortment of room papers, window shades, Turcoman draperies, Nottingham and Irish point lace curtains, Madras curtains, drapery poles, etc. Mr. Cook makes a specialty of house furnishings, and no one in need of goods in that line can fail to satisfy themselves at his establishment. Draperies of special designs to match carpets and furniture will be ordered from the largest houses in Boston and New York at short notice. Mr. Cook has had several years' experience in the musical instrument trade, and anyone in want of a piano or organ can save money by consulting him. The enterprise in question was started in 1889 by the present proprietor, who is a native of Maine. Competent assistants are employed and a prosperous retail business is done. Mr. Cook has shown both liberality and foresight in the management of his business, and fully deserves his success.

WM. C. DONNELL, Insurance Agent, Market

Square, Houlton, Me.—There are few insurance agencies in this section of the State that can show such a record as that held by the one carried on by Mr. Wm. C. Donnell on Market square, for although this agency has been under the management of its present proprietor only fifteen years, the amount of business now done will compare favorably with that transacted by many concerns of much longer standing. The cause of this exceptional success is no secret, for business men are quick to appreciate able and faithful service, and it is generally conceded that no insurance agency in Houlton is more prompt and painstaking in looking after the interests of its patrons. Then, again, the list of companies represented is unsurpassed, for there is not one of them but what has proved itself worthy of absolute confidence, and some of the leading foreign companies are acted for as well as the most prominent home organizations. We give the list below, and are sure that our readers will agree that what we have said concerning it, is fully justified by the facts. It is as follows: Home Insurance Co. of New York; Niagara Insurance Co. of New York, American Insurance Co. of New York; National Insurance Co. of Hartford, Conn.; Orient Insurance Co. of Hartford, Conn.; Springfield Insurance Co. of Springfield, Mass.; Imperial Insurance Co. of London, Eng.; City of London Insurance Co. of London, Eng.; Guardian Insurance Co. of London, Eng.; Fire Insurance Co. of Philadelphia, Pa.; People's Insurance Co. of Manchester, N. H.; Merchants Insurance Co. of Newark, N. J.; California Insurance Co. of San Francisco, Cal.; Mechanics and Traders Insurance Co. of New Orleans, La. Mr. Donnell is prepared to effect insurance to any amount, and promptly adjust and pay losses at his office. He is a native of Houlton, and is cashier of the First National Bank of this town. He is widely known in this vicinity, and is regarded as competent authority in all insurance matters.

THE RAYMOND CO., dealers in Crockery,

Glass, Tin and Silverware, 5 and 10 Cent Goods. Manufacturers of all kinds of Hair Work, Court St., Houlton, Me.

This company was originally started by Mr. L. C. Raymond, who was succeeded in 1886 by The A. H. Raymond Company, and who in 1890 was succeeded by The Raymond Co., and is at the present time known as the Raymond Co.

The establishment occupied is centrally located, and covers an area of some 1200 square feet, and is under the general management of Lewis C. Raymond.

First Department.

Is the manufacturing of human hair goods, such as switches, puffs, curls, frizzes, and wigs, for both ladies and gents. Mrs. Raymond is one of the finest workwomen this side of Europe, and has had some eighteen years experience in the business. Orders are received from all parts of the States, and as far south as Stewart, Va. Prices are within the reach of all and orders by mail will receive prompt attention.

Second Department.

House furnishing goods, such as crockery, glass, tin and silverware, notions, jewelry, five and ten cent counters.

Third Department.

Furniture, organs, sewing machines, sold for cash, or on the installment plan. A good big discount for all cash buyers, that will surprise them, so that they will almost jump out of their shoes.

Fourth Department.

Organs and sewing machines cleaned and repaired at lowest living prices.

Fifth Department.

General commission merchants, in selling all kinds of goods. Court street, Houlton, Me.

L. MONSON & SON, dealers in Meats and Groceries; also, "Our Own Make" Fine Sausage, Proprietors of West End Bakery. All goods delivered free of charge. Houlton, Me.—In collecting information relating to the leading business men of Houlton, it very soon became manifest that Messrs. L. Monson & Son, would have to be included in any account of such, for evidences were found on every side to indicate that these gentlemen were fairly entitled to the honor, and that as regards enterprise and popularity, they occupy a high position in the trade circle. The enterprise now conducted by them was originally established in 1865 by Mr. L. Monson, and in 1888, his son, Mr. A. B. Monson, was admitted to the business, since which date the firm-name has been L. Monson & Son. A most extensive and flourishing retail trade has been built up, and premises of the dimensions of 30×65 feet are occupied. Meats and groceries of all kinds are handled, and whether any or both of these commodities are wanted, this establishment will be found a most desirable place at which to procure the same, as the assortment is large, the quality excellent, and the prices low. In addition to their retail meat and grocery trade, Messrs. Monson & Son make a fine grade of sausage, and are the proprietors of the West End Bakery. Three competent and courteous assistants are employed, and those who may favor these gentlemen with their patronage will have every reason to cordially subscribe to all that we have stated, concerning their business methods, for their motto, "Good goods at reasonable prices," is strictly lived up to. Messrs. L. and A. B Monson are both natives of Houlton, and Mr. L. Monson served in the army during our late Southern war.

HIRAM SMITH & CO., dealers in Flour, Grain, Mill Feeds, Groceries. Teas, Coffees, etc.; Corn of all kinds a specialty: Houlton, Me.—The prices of such standard commodities as those handled by Messrs. Hiram Smith & Co., do not vary at different stores so much as do those quoted on less staple articles, but there is apt to be a variation in quality if not in price, and therefore it is well to obtain them from a dealer who is reputable as well as enterprising. Mr. Smith, the senior partner, is a native of Phillips, Maine. He founded his present business at Houlton in 1888, and has built up a large retail trade, being prepared to fill the heaviest orders at short notice. The premises occupied are centrally located and comprise two floors, each measuring some 1500 square feet, which contain an immense stock of flour, grain and mill feeds, as well as groceries, teas, coffees, etc., these goods being of guaranteed quality and quoted at the lowest prevailing rates. Mr. Smith makes a specialty of corn of all kinds, and those requiring flour for family use would do well to place an order with him, for he handles the most popular brands, and the goods will surely give satisfaction. All orders by mail will receive as immediate and careful attention as those given in person. We would, therefore, advise those who have not already done so, to call at this establishment and inspect the goods and prices.

I. W. GOULD, dealer in Groceries and Provisions, Houlton, Me.—We confess that we don't know how long the store now occupied by Mr. I. W. Gould, at Houlton has been utilized for the sale of groceries and provisions, for it was founded by Mr. J. L. Carney, who was succeeded by Mr. Gould, but we do know that its present genial proprietor has been in possession since 1878. Under Mr. Gould's liberal and skillful management, however, the establishment has attained a popularity that it never knew before, and to those who want first-class groceries and provisions, and prompt and courteous attention, we would say that here is the place to get them. Mr. Gould was born in Brownville, Me., and is well known throughout Houlton and vicinity. He has worked hard to build up his present business and certainly deserves all the patronage he receives. He occupies well arranged premises and employs active and competent assistants, and is in a position to promise satisfactory service to all. The stock carried is one that would do honor to a much more pretentious establishment, for it is complete in every detail and comprises a fine assortment of staple and fancy groceries, and a full assortment of provisions of all kinds. Family flour is of course very largely handled and is supplied by the bag or barrel at prices that cannot fail to please.

HISTORICAL SKETCH OF CARIBOU.

It is a favorite saying that Caribou has as much energy to the square inch as any other town in the United States, and when we consider that Caribou has grown more rapidly than any other large Aroostook town and bear in mind the fact that the growth of Aroostook County in population and valuation within the past decade has been so phenomenal as to have challenged the attention of the nation, it is not at all difficult to accept that saying as the plain, unvarnished truth. The residents of Caribou are not only energetic, but are public-spirited and united also, and as they have the most implicit confidence in the future of their town they do not hesitate to vote large sums of money for the development of local resources. Many practical examples of their liberality in this respect might be cited but one will suffice, and that the voting of $2,000 per year for twenty years to secure the building of a dam across the Aroostook River. This is an enormous outlay for such a town as Caribou but it is that kind of liberality which is really the truest economy and it furnishes an impressive rebuke to the "penny wise and pound foolish" policy which is the curse of too many New England communities. Many substantial advantages have already been gained by the building of this dam and if any of Caribou's residents had doubts of the wisdom of its construction they must already have been dissipated. As this is by far the most important of the public works carried out in Caribou up to the present time, we will refer to it in detail in another portion of this sketch.

The location of Caribou has been described as "very remote and yet extremely favorable" and there is considerable justice in this description, although so far as "remoteness" is concerned Caribou's location is superior to that of many other Aroostook towns, its possession of railway facilities bringing it practically much nearer the great distributing and trade centres than many towns considerably nearer to them, reckoning by actual distance. Caribou is situated in the northeastern part of Aroostook County and is bounded on the north by Connor, on the east by Limestone and Fort Fairfield, on the south by Presque Isle, and on the west by New Sweden, Woodland and Washburn. It is 54 miles north-northwest of Houlton and is the terminus of a stage route from that town, via Presque Isle, stage lines running also to New Sweden, Van Buren and Perham. Caribou is on the New Brunswick Railway, and being at the extremity of the long loop-formed by that road in its line from Presque Isle to Fort Fairfield is about midway between those points by rail. Its area is the same as that of those towns, both being double townships and Caribou comprising what were formerly Forestville Plantation and Lyndon, or "II" and "I" townships and Eaton grant. The town is twelve miles long and six miles wide, and its surface, soil and climate are all highly favorable to agriculture, Caribou being one of the best farming towns in the country. It is in the centre of a vast and highly productive agricultural region and profits by that fact both directly and indirectly although the present profit is but an earnest of what may reasonably be expected in the near future. The township is excellently watered and contains many valuable water powers in addition to the truly magnificent one afforded by the damming of the Aroostook River. This stream enters the township at a point near its southeast corner, passes up through the southern half to the centre of the town, then turns abruptly to the southeast and passes out, crossing the eastern boundary line at a point a little south of its middle. Caribou Stream flows into the town from the west and empties into the Aroostook River at Caribou Village, near the centre of the town, while the Little Madawaska River enters the township from New Sweden, passes out into Connor on the north, re-enters Caribou after making a small loop and flows east and then south, finally joining the Aroostook River a short distance from Caribou's eastern boundary. Both the Caribou and the Madawaska furnish excellent power for saw, shingle, grist and woolen mills, and their waters have been utilized for such purposes for many years, the first grist and saw mills having been built in 1844, a year after the settlement of the town. It is said that the Caribou Stream is made to do as much work as any water-course of its size in the State, and this may readily be believed, there being four dams across it within a distance of a half a mile from the village. There are excellent mill privileges on the Little Madawaska River, some two miles east of the village. Mills have also been located on Otter Brook and there are other small streams capable of affording power to a limited extent. But all the small water powers in town are as nothing compared with that furnished by the damming of the Aroostook River, this being conceded to be the finest water power in the country, east of the Penobscot River. We have referred to the great enterprise, determination and confidence exhibited by the residents of Caribou in pledging $2,000 a year for twenty years to secure this vastly important public improvement and a brief description of it may properly be given in order that non-residents may be able to form some idea of what Caribou is doing to promote her interests and attract manufacturers. The following facts are official having been furnished by Mr. II. M. Heath, business manager of the company that furnished the dam and the water works. We copy from the *Industrial Journal* of Bangor, — a paper that has done and is doing much to promote the interests of this section :

"The dam was built by Thos. J. Emery of Waterville, a veteran at the business. It is 500 feet long, 14 feet high and 48 feet wide at base. It is constructed of hemlock in lower part and cedar above with hackmatack gates and gateways. The entire dam is planked with six inch birch plank 600,000 feet of hemlock logs were used and from 800,000 to 900,000 feet of lumber in all, also 15,000 tons of ballast and 40 tons of iron. There are six gates, three on each side of the river, with protection piers at each end. One end of the dam is bedded to the ledge, and the other extends into the bank 50 feet. The dam is most thoroughly and substantially built and makes the finest water power east of the Penobscot River. It is perfectly safe to say that an average horse power of more than 3,000 is secured, as by actual computation at the time of the test, above 7,000 horse power was running over the dam. This is ample for any and all purposes, and pulp mills, lumber mills, cotton or woolen mills, with numberless smaller manufactories can be driven from this dam. The pond made by this dam is six miles long, and the New Brunswick Railway, which runs along by the side of the river has had to be graded up from two to four feet for nearly that distance. The New Brunswick Railway Co., has offered to put in side tracks for any manufactory established on the east side of the river, and if manufactories should be established on the west side, they would cross the river for their accommodation. The railway now passes within 100 feet of the dam. On the west side there is a plateau below the dam one-half mile long and 600 feet wide, most admirably adapted for the establishment of manufactories."

THE WATER POWER OF CARIBOU.

The dam was completed in 1880, and the fact that seventy-five new buildings were erected in Caribou Village that year shows that private and public enterprise go hand in hand. The village is very favorably situated for a system of water works and those now in use were furnished by the same parties who built the dam, and as regards reliability and efficiency are unsurpassed in the entire State. The entire plant cost about $100,000 of which $35,000 represents the cost of the dam alone. Most of the village lies in the valley of Caribou Stream and to the north of it is a hill more than 200 feet high, this being the site of the standpipe, which is thirty feet in diameter, twenty-nine feet high and has a capacity of 150,000 gallons. It is about three-quarters of a mile from the pumping station at the dam and is connected there with an eight inch iron main pipe; the other main pipes being six inches in diameter. Numerous hydrants are located throughout the village and so well arranged that four or five streams can be thrown on to any business block. An impressive showing of the efficiency of the water works as a means of protection against loss by fire was made at a public exhibition given shortly after their completion. The fire alarm was sounded and in less than two minutes five streams were directed towards King Block, just ninety seconds having passed from the time of the giving of the alarm. Five steady streams were thrown fifty feet above the roof of the block and with a pressure of 100 pounds horizontal streams were thrown 187 feet by actual measurement, while the perpendicular streams were estimated to rise fully 150 feet. The aggregate quantity of water thrown was something immense, and it is difficult to conceive of a fire in any Caribou building that could not be promptly and effectually squelched by the means now at the disposal of the town. A Holmes water wheel furnishes the motive power for the pumps, which was furnished by the George F. Blake Manufacturing Company, of Boston. It is duplex, has twelve-inch cylinders, eight-inch main and six-inch pipe and has a nominal capacity of 1,000,000 gallons in 24 hours, but can furnish half as much again if necessary. The water wheel is rated at 140 horse power but only about one half that amount is required to supply water enough for present consumption. This large reserve of power and the uniform reliability of the water works up to the present time under all circumstances, amply justify the confidence reposed in the system and reflects the highest credit on the skill and judgment of those who devised and constructed it. From a sanitary as well as from an economic point of view the importance of an abundant supply of pure running water can scarcely be over-estimated and the citizens of Caribou may well congratulate themselves on the excellence of the service they enjoy. The fire department is thoroughly organized, well equipped with hose and so forth, of the most improved type, and excellently managed. Mr. H. D. Collins being the efficient chief engineer. It is to be hoped that a long time will elapse before its mettle will be tried by any serious conflagration but there is every reason to believe that it will render a good account of itself even under the most unfavorable circumstances.

Of course Caribou possesses a first class electric-light plant, for it would be strange indeed if so enterprising a community had failed to avail itself of the many advantages of the modern illuminant. The Caribou Electric Light Company utilizes the Mather incandescent system and supplies several hundred lights, the larger stores etc., of the village being brilliantly illuminated. The standing of the town as a trade centre is already high and local trale interests are steadily developing, for the advantages possessed by Caribou merchants enable them to offer inducements which draw custom from all the country adjacent, and no small share of their success in this respect is due to the legitimate and honorable methods followed, "full value for money received" being the foundation upon which their trade has been established. The leading commercial and industrial enterprises of the town are treated of in detail in the pages following this sketch and a careful reading of the articles in question will enable orders to be placed more intelligently and to better advantage than would otherwise be possible. Caribou is one of the principal shipping points for potatoes and shingles, and a goodly proportion of the out of town trade enjoyed by local houses is due to this fact. With the further development of the almost unlimited resources of the adjacent country and the great improvement in railway facilities which is sure to be made before many years. the shipments at Caribou will reach so immense an amount that those of the past and present, large as they have been and are, will seem insignificant by comparison; and it is also an indisputable fact that direct railway communication over American soil to tide-water will act powerfully and quickly in the development of Caribous' manufacturing possibilities. As yet these have not begun to be availed of on any large scale, for although there are varied and important manufactures carried on in the town the wide field open here is so sparsely occupied as to seem almost empty. The more important Caribou industries include the manufacture of starch, lumber, doors, sash and blinds, woolen goods, carriages, flour and meal, harnesses, clothing, cheese, etc., and there are also well equipped foundries and machine shops, blacksmiths' shops, etc. There is an excellent opening here for one or more of the great pulp mills now being established throughout New England in general and Maine in particular and lumber, cotton, woolen and other mills could be established here under favorable conditions, the townspeople individually and as a community being prepared to warmly welcome such enterprises and give them all reasonable aid, while the railway company will lay sidings free of expense and spare no pains to furnish satisfactory transportation facilities. In this connection it is pertinent to note that there is an energetic Board of Trade in Caribou, made up of representative business men, and ready and willing to meet any responsible party half-way in enterprises calculated to add to the prosperity of the community as a whole. Mr. Albe Holmes is president, and Mr. Calvin B. Roberts is secretary of this organization, and capitalists and others wishing absolutely reliable information concerning the business opportunities at Caribou may obtain it by corresponding with the latter gentlemen, all communications addressed to C. B. Roberts, Secretary Board of Trade, Caribou, Maine, being assured immediate and painstaking attention. There is none of that pettiness and small jealousy in Caribou which hinders the development of far too many communities, the leading business men being united in their efforts to advance the common interests of the town and fully appreciating the fact that there is room enough and to spare for all practical men having capital and brains who may choose to identify themselves with this enterprising community.

The towns-people are sociable as well as energetic and industrious, and there are various associations in town including several Masonic Societies, an Odd Fellow Lodge, a Grand Army Post, and several fraternal organizations such as the Knights of Pythias and the New England Order of Protection. Another and still stronger advantage offered by Caribou as a place of residence is that afforded by the excellence of the local schools, they being very liberally supported and being unsurpassed in point of practical efficiency by any in eastern Maine. They are very largely attended also, the number of

THE NEW HIGH SCHOOL.

scholars being larger than that of any other town in the county. The High School building erected in 1890 at an expense of $14,000 is a model edifice of the kind and the school itself is one in which every public spirited citizen may well take pride, the principal, W. S. Knowlton, A. M., being one of Maine's leading educators, and the course of instruction being comprehensive, valuable and practical in the true sense of that much abused word. The local religious societies include organizations of Baptists, Free Baptists, Congregationalists, Methodists, Universalists, Episcopalians and Catholics, and prominent among the church edifices is St. Luke's Episcopal Church, erected several years ago and having seating accommodations for 150. It is a tastefully designed and well constructed building 25 x 55 feet in dimensions.

We have several times referred to the high position held by Caribou as a farming town and the subject is of sufficient importance to warrant our giving a few details concerning it, especially as the mere statement that agriculture is extensively and profitably carried on here will convey but little idea of the true condition of affairs to those familiar with ordinary New England farming. The prevailing rock within the township is limestone, and the soil is a dark, rich loom which yields heavy crops of potatoes, wheat and oats. Aroostook County potatoes are far too widely and favorably known to need any eulogy in these columns, and if any one doubts that there is money to be made by their intelligent cultivation he makes a most decided mistake, as will be seen by the following examples of what has actually been done in this line : Mr. J. B. Southerland lives about three miles from Caribou Village and is one of those farmers who believe that farming, like all other industries, is a progressive art and that hard and intelligent effort and liberal but judicious expenditures are essential to pronounced success in it. In 1890 he sold from thirteen acres of land $1300 worth of potatoes, besides using all required by his own family and putting aside enough to plant fifteen acres. After paying for phosphate, labor, etc., he had $800 left as the net income from that thirteen acres of land. Another enterprising and successful farmer is Mr. E. A. Goodwin, who lives four miles from Caribou Village. In 1890 he sold 1900 barrels of potatoes from nineteen acres of land for $2,500. He saved 90 barrels for seed and after paying all bills found that he had cleared about $1500. Certainly that kind of farming pays; there is no reason why men should toil from sunrise to sunset on the stony hill-farms of New England to gain a bare livelihood when such opportunities are open to them in Caribou and vicinity.

The growth of that town since its incorporation, April 5, 1859, has been rapid and of late years wonderfully so, it having nearly doubled during the past decade while its valuation considerably more than doubled. In 1870 the population was 1,410 ; in 1880, 2,756, and in 1890, 4,087 ; while in 1870 the valuation was $155,702; in 1880, $337,388; and in 1890, $780,439. These figures are obtained from official sources and are therefore as reliable as such figures can be, and they tell the story of Caribou's development so plainly and completely that they form a most fitting conclusion to this brief sketch of one of the most promising towns in by far the most rapidly developing county of the Pine Tree State.

Representative Business Men of Caribou, Me.

AROOSTOOK TRUST AND BANKING CO.

Required and Paid-up Capital, $50,000; Authorized Capital, $1,000,000; Caribou, Me.—The Aroostook Trust and Banking Company was incorporated by special act of the legislature in 1889, as a result of the efforts of several energetic business men and public spirited citizens actuated by the conviction that this section of the State was in need of additional banking facilities and that such facilities could best be furnished by an association of men thoroughly identified with local enterprises and thoroughly conversant with local needs and resources. The simple fact that the valuation of Aroostook county has nearly doubled during the past ten years is of itself enough to show that a phenomenally rapid development is going on and that it is the part of wisdom not to depend upon facilities, excellent in their time and excellent now so far as they go, but quite inadequate to accommodate the demands of the present day. In short, the idea of the promoters of this company was to provide a service which should supplement and not supersede that previously enjoyed, a service capable of great expansion, comprehensive in its scope, well considered in every detail, and of so efficient a character as to be assured the support of all classes. The company has a required and paid up capital of $50,000 and is authorized to increase it to $1,000,000, so that it is thoroughly well prepared to extend its operations as occasion may require and to easily keep pace with the rapidly increasing demand which is a necessary consequence of the constant development practically assured to this section of the State by existing conditions. The company is empowered to do a general banking business, to act as agent and trustee for corporations and individuals, and to execute legal trusts. Every accommodation, consistent with prudent banking, is extended to its customers and it enjoys the confidence and support of the public to an exceptional degree. The representative character of the institution may be judged from the following list of officers: president and treasurer, George I. Trickey; vice president, J. Cary, M. D.; secretary, C. B. Margosson. Trustees: George I. Trickey, J. Cary, M. D., S. W. Collins, L. C. Stearns, L. W. Sawin, W. C. Spaulding, Samuel Taylor, John P. Donworth, W. H. Gray.

W. C. SPAULDING, dealer in Hardware,

Paints and Oils, Iron, Steel, Stoves and Tin Ware, Glass, Sash and Doors, Caribou, Me.—In every city or town there are certain mercantile enterprises which by reason of their long standing, able management and high reputation are conceded by all to hold the leading position in their special line, and just such an enterprise is that conducted by Mr. W. C. Spaulding. He is a native of Buckfield, Me., and is to-day unquestionably one of the best-known men in the county in both business and social circles. Mr. Spaulding has held the position of town clerk, and has been engaged in active business here in Caribou for about a score of years, having inaugurated his present enterprise in 1872. He is a dealer in hardware, paints and oils, iron, steel, stoves and tin ware, glass, sash and doors, and some idea of the magnitude of the business and the size of the stock carried may be gained from the fact that the premises made use of comprise three floors, each 26×105 feet in dimensions, giving a total floor-space of more than 8000 square feet. The assortment of the various articles we have mentioned is exceptionally complete and as the goods (especially the paints and oils) are very carefully selected and obtained from the most reliable sources, they will give the best of satisfaction, as indeed is well known to all who have placed orders with this representative house. Employment is given to four assistants, and both large as well as small orders are assured prompt as well as careful attention.

S. W. COLLINS & SON, Manufacturers of and

dealers in Long and Short Lumber, and General Merchandise, Caribou, Me.—It is nearly half a century since the business now carried on by Messrs. S. W. Collins & Son was founded, operations having been begun in 1844 by Messrs. Vaughn & Collins. In 1858, Mr. S. W. Collins became sole proprietor, and subsequently the firm of Collins & Porter was formed, the present concern being organized in 1879. It is constituted of Messrs. S. W. and H. D. Collins, the former a native of Bangor and the latter of this town, and both being so widely known throughout this section as to render further mention quite unnecessary. The firm manufacture long and short lumber, and deal in grain, feed and general merchandise, their facilities being such as to enable them to fill both large and small orders without delay and at positively the lowest market rates. They operate a steam grist and shingle mill and also a long lumber mill, and employ from eighteen to twenty-five assistants. Their store is 25×74 feet in dimensions, and all available space is fully utilized, the stock of general merchandise being extremely large and exceptionally complete in every department, the goods composing it being obtained from the best reliable sources and guaranteed to prove precisely as represented in every respect. Both partners give the business close personal attention, and spare no pains to maintain the enviable reputation so long associated with it.

IRVING & RICKER,

DEALERS IN

Country Produce, Farming Tools,

WAGONS, SAND, LIME, BRICK, ETC.

CARIBOU, ME.

C. M. RUNNELS, Fire, Life and Accident Insurance, Main Street, Caribou, Me.—The question of where and how insurance may be placed to the best advantage is one that appeals directly to every adult member of the community, for every owner of insurable property should most certainly protect himself against loss by fire, and those who own no house, factory, store, furniture or stock of goods have special reason for insuring their life in order to protect those dependent upon them. We don't propose to argue in favor of insurance but simply to give our readers a hint how to obtain it to the best advantage and hence we call their attention at once to the facilities offered by Mr. C. M. Runnels, doing business on Main street. He is prepared to place fire insurance to any desired amount in standard companies, and to issue life and accident policies which are liberal in their provisions and absolute in the protection they afford. Full information will cheerfully be given by him on application in person or by mail, and all commissions will be promptly executed at uniformly moderate rates.

DR. BARKER, Dentist, Caribou, Me.—That it pays to take care of the teeth is a fact that every one learns by experience sooner or later, but unfortunately many do not learn it until their teeth have become so seriously injured that the most that can be done is to "patch them up" more or less perfectly. But the principle "better late than never" applies with especial force to the care of the teeth, for in the present advanced stage of dental science much can be done to preserve impaired, and restore or replace badly injured teeth, and hence, such of our readers as have been careless or dilatory in this respect should delay no longer, but submit themselves to the treatment of a skilled and well-equipped dentist, and in this connection we may properly call attention to the service offered by Dr. Barker of Caribou, for he is an expert and reliable practitioner, gentle but thorough in his methods, moderate in his charges, and possessing all necessary facilities to practice dentistry in all its branches in accordance with the most approved principles and means. Appointments may be made in advance, thus ensuring against disappointment and delay, and parties living out of town would do well to make arrangements by mail, as by so doing they will be spared unnecessary travelling and serve their own interests in every way.

J. A. AKERSTROM, Manufacturer of and dealer in Harness and Horse Furnishings, Caribou, Me.—There are some things that every man has to find out for himself as the experience of others doesn't seem to help him at all, and among these things is the fact that it doesn't pay to buy inferior harness no matter how low a price may be quoted on it. Of course it doesn't pay to give fancy prices for even the best harness, but it most certainly does pay to give a fair price for honest goods and if you want such goods at as low prices as can be named on them, just place your order with Mr. J. A.

Akerstrom and you will get them every time. Mr. Akerstrom is a native of Sweden, and has had long experience in the harness business. He was a member of the firm of Akerstrom Brothers, who succeeded Mr. E. E. Farrell in 1889, and he became sole proprietor in 1891. He is a manufacturer of as well as dealer in harness and horse furnishings, and is prepared to make harness to order or do repairing neatly and strongly at short notice and at low rates. An assortment of harnesses and horse furnishings is always carried in stock, and the goods are not only sold at low rates but guaranteed to prove just as represented.

A. M. YORK, Agricultural Tools, Sweden Street, Caribou, Me.—It is said that " a good workman is known by his tools," and this rule holds good in the case of the farmer as well as in that of the mechanic, for it is very rarely that an enterprising, progressive and successful farmer is found using inferior tools, provided, of course, that first class tools are obtainable. There is certainly no difficulty in obtaining them in this section, and what is still more important, in obtaining them at the lowest market rates, for by placing your order with Mr. A. M. York you can get agricultural tools of every description, made by the leading manufacturers and fully warranted in every respect, at prices as low as the lowest. This fact is very generally known hereabouts and as it is also known that Mr. York fills orders promptly as well as carefully it is not surprising that he should do an extensive business. He is agent for the Walter A. Wood harvesting machines and A. W. Gray's Sons threshing machines ; also Soluble Pacific Guano. His store is located on Sweden street, and such of our readers as propose buying any kind of farming tools will best serve their own interests by visiting this establishment before placing an order.

MRS. A. L. IRELAND, Millinery and Fancy Goods, Sweden Street, Caribou, Me.—The establishment conducted by Mrs. A. L. Ireland is very popular among the ladies of this vicinity, and its popularity is apparently equally great among those who trim their own hats and bonnets and those who prefer to entrust that work to others, the reason being that Mrs. Ireland caters very successfully to both classes of trade, she carrying a large and most skillfully chosen stock of trimmed and untrimmed hats and bonnets, ribbons, feathers, velvets, laces and millinery goods in general, besides a full line of fancy goods, and being prepared to do millinery work to order in the most artistic manner at short notice and at reasonable rates. She is a native of New York State, and has carried on her present establishment about five years, having assumed possession in 1886. The premises occupied are located on Sweden street, and have an area of about 1000 square feet. The latest fashionable novelties may always be found here, and the prices quoted are uniformly moderate, while the service is very prompt and efficient, employment being given to two assistants.

J. A. CLARK,

DEALER IN

DRY GOODS, BOOTS AND SHOES, ETC.,

CARIBOU, MAINE.

Mr. J. A. Clark has been an active and successful merchant here in Caribou for a number of years and now carries on what is conceded to be the leading establishment of the kind in this section, but he is even more widely and favorably known than these facts would seem to indicate for Mr. Clark is prominent in public as well as in business life, he having served as representative and as senator, and now being United States pension agent for Maine. He is a native of Corinna, Me., and served in the army during the Rebellion, with the rank of captain. The business with which he is identified was founded about fourteen years ago by Messrs. G. S. Clark & Co., the present proprietor having had entire control about five years. The store has an area of about 1000 square feet and contains a stock of dry goods, boots and shoes, etc.,

that must truly "be seen to be appreciated," for it is exceptionally desirable, both on account of the dependable quality of the goods it comprises and the attractiveness and freshness of the styles it includes. A "shopping" trip to Caribou would be considered sadly incomplete did it not include a visit to this popular store, for the public in general and the ladies in particular agree that the attractions here offered are in many respects unparalleled elsewhere. The very latest novelties in dress goods are always well represented, while the assortment of ladies' and childrens' furnishings is such as is seldom found outside a large city. Dependable foot-wear is another leading specialty and the stock is so complete that all feet can be fitted and all tastes and purses suited.

C. JENSEN, Watchmaker, and Manufacturing Jeweler, Caribou, Me.—Those who agree that a man cannot know too much about the articles in which he deals will support us in the assertion that it is always best to buy of the manufacturer if possible, and this is particularly true where jewelry is concerned, for reasons so plain and obvious as not to require mention. Hence those wishing anything in the line of jewelry, watches, etc., should place the order with Mr. C. Jensen, for he is a watch maker and manufacturing jeweler, and, although of course, he doesn't make all the articles he sells, still, he knows more about them than could possibly be known by one ignorant of the trade, as the majority of those who call themselves jewelers are. Many of our readers have doubtless learned by sad experience that it is difficult to get a fine watch properly repaired and cleaned, and they will thank us for calling their attention to Mr. Jensen's facilities, for these are of the best, and as he is an expert workman, we can guarantee satisfaction to every customer. He is a native of Sweden, and has made many friends in Caribou and vicinity by his accommodating methods and evident desire to deal honorably with all his customers. He deals in crockery and lamp goods, as well as in watches, jewelry, etc., and quotes the lowest market rates on articles of warranted merit.

H. E. JONES, dealer in Crockery, Glassware, Stoneware and Lamp Goods, Paper Hangings and Curtains, Jewelry, Silverware, Spectacles, Eye Glasses and Fishing Tackle; American Watch Repairing a specialty; Holmes Block, Caribou, Me.—There is not a more attractive store in town than that carried on by Mr. H. E. Jones in Holmes Block, for the stock is very carefully selected, is admirably arranged, and comprises a great variety of goods that are ornamental as well as useful. And those who believe that "handsome is that handsome does" will find this store doubly attractive, for it is the home of low prices, so that its attractions can be availed of by all purses as well as by all tastes. Mr. Jones deals in crockery, glassware, stoneware and lamp goods, paper hangings and curtains, jewelry, silverware, spectacles, eye glasses and fishing tackle, carrying a full line of each of these commodities, and constantly renewing his assortment so that it always includes the latest novelties. He has carried on the establishment since 1884, and the public have long since learned that goods bought here prove just as represented, and that full value is given for every dollar received. A specialty is made of American watch repairing, the work being skillfully done at very short notice, and moderate charges being made in every case.

WILLIAM ROBINSON, Shingle Mill, Caribou, Me.—The manufacture of Shingles is one of the most important industries carried on in this section of the State and is destined to remain so for many years to come and to develop steadily until it has reached much greater magnitude even than is now the case. Therefore it is very appropriate that it should be given prominent mention in such a book as this, and in making such mention it would never do to pass over the shingle mill carried on by Mr. William Robinson, this being a representative establishment of its kind. It has been conducted by Mr. Robinson for about three years and gives employment to from ten to fifteen hands; containing two machines of the most improved type which are run by water power. The product is very uniform in quality in the several grades, and is large enough to enable the heaviest orders to be filled at short notice, the lowest market rates being quoted at all times.

LITTLEFIELD & CO., Fine Custom Tailoring, and manufacturers of Ready-Made Clothing, Gentlemen's Furnishing Goods, and Hats and Caps a Specialty, Sweden Street, Caribou, Me.—It is but seldom that we have occasion to mention an establishment that we can so heartily and confidently recommend to all classes of purchasers as we can that conducted by Messrs Littlefield & Co., and located on Sweden street, for there are but very few establishments that cater so intelligently and successfully to both those who have much and those who have little to spend, to those who prefer custom-made clothing and those who find ready-made clothing satisfactory. Of course, because a man wears ready-made clothing it by no means follows that he can't afford custom made garments, and indeed many buy both—ready-made for working and general wear and custom-made for dress wear—but what we want to say is that no matter how much or how little you propose to spend for clothing you cannot possibly spend it to better advantage than at this deservedly popular store, for Messrs. Littlefield & Co., not only do fine custom tailoring but are also manufacturers of ready-made clothing and carry a stock varied enough to enable all forms to be fitted and all tastes to be suited. They also carry a heavy and complete stock of gentlemen's furnishing goods, and hats and caps, embracing the latest fashionable novelties and offered at bottom prices. The store is spacious and conveniently arranged, and sufficient assistance is employed to ensure prompt and careful attention to every caller.

W. H. FISHER,

Attorney and Counselor at Law,

CARIBOU, - MAINE.

—

ISAAC COCHRAN, Boarding House, Livery and Feed Stable, Blacksmithing, Caribou, Me.—A m o n g the various busin ss enterprises carried on in Caribou those conducted by Mr. Isaac Cochran deserve prominent and favorable mention, on account of their popularity and the efficiency and reliability of their management. Mr Cochran was born in this town, and is extremely well known throughout this vicinity as an energetic and honorable business man. He carries on a boarding house, a livery and feed stable, and a blacksmith shop, and employs suffi ient assistance to enable him to offer prompt and efficient service at all times. Mr. Cochran's stable contains twenty-four stalls, and during the season a large livery business is done, as satisfactory teams are furnished at very reasonable rates, and at short notice. Horses boarded here are assured good food, comfortable quarters and the best of care. In the blacksmith shop special attention is given to horse shoeing, but jobbing of all kinds will also be done in a superior manner, and at moderate rates. The boarding house is too well and favorably known to need any praise in these columns, and we will only add that Mr. Cochran gives careful personal attention to all of the enterprises with which he is connected.

—

E. P. GRIMES, General Merchandise and Sawed and Shaved Shingles, Caribou, Me.—The term "general merchandise" is so indefinite that but little idea of the character of the stock carried by a dealer, can be gained from the simple statement that he handles "general merchandise," the only thing surely indicated being that he confines himself to no particular branch of trade. But when used in connection with the business carried on by Mr E P. Grimes, the term should be interpreted in its broadest sense. for his stock comprises full lines of building material, lime, brick, etc., etc., dry goods, groceries, boots and shoes, hardware, agricultural tools. crockery and tinware, and notions, and as it is constantly being renewed it always includes many late and attractive novelties. Mr. Grimes was born in Lawrence, Mass., and has carried on his present enterprise about nine years, during which time it has gained a popularity second to that of no other in this vicinity. The store is located on Vaughan street, and is 40×80 feet in dimensions, spacious storerooms also being utilized. Considering the magnitude and completeness of the stock it is hardly necessary to say that all classes of trade are catered to and all tastes can be suited, and we may add that the prices are invaria bly as low as the lowest on all the commodities dealt in. Mr. Grimes also deals largely in sawed and shaved shingles, employs from forty to fifty assistants, and is prepared to fill all orders at short notice and at bottom rates.

THE CARIBOU DRUG STORE, S. L. White, Apothecary, Main Street, Caribou, Me.—The "Caribou Drug Store" has a more than local reputation, for it is patronized by residents of all the country adjacent to the town, and it well deserves its popularity; first, because of the absolute reliability of the service rendered; second, because of the promptness with which customers are served; and third, because of the lowness of the prices quoted in every department of the business. This store was carried on about fifteen years before the present proprietor, Mr. S. L. White, assumed control in 1887. He is a native of St. Johns, N. B , and is not only an experienced and skillful apothecary, but is exceptionally careful in his methods, the result being that the public have the utmost confidence in him, knowing that prescriptions placed in his hands will be accurately compounded from the purest materials obtainable. He carries a large stock of drugs, medicines and chemicals, and compounds prescriptions at as low rates as are consistent with the use of the best ingredients. Two prominent specialties of Mr. White's manufacture are *White's Condition Powders* and *White's White Pine Expectorant*, both of which have gained a large sale. A stock of toilet and fancy articles, books and stationery, artists' materials, etc., is also carried, low prices being quoted on all the articles it comprises, and prompt and careful attention being assured to every caller by the employment of two competent assistants.

—

SAMUEL TAYLOR & SON, Starch Manufacturers and dealers in Groceries and Provisions, Boots and Shoes, Dry Goods, etc., Lumbermen's and Farmer's Supplies a Specialty, Caribou, Me.—If a stranger in Caribou were to ask the first person he met on the street where he could place an order for groceries and provisions, boots and shoes, dry goods, etc., and be sure of having it promptly and satisfactorily filled at low rates, he would probably be directed to the establishment conducted by Messrs. Samuel Taylor & Son, for these gentlemen are universally known and highly popular. This is not at all surprising, for the senior partner has been in business here since 1878 and has always made it a rule to deal liberally and fairly by his customers, to give them an opportunity to choose from a very large and complete stock, to sell all goods strictly on their merits and to quote bottom prices on all the commodities dealt in. Both members of the firm are natives of Burlington, Me., and are universally known in Caribou and vicinity, in social as well as in business circles. Mr. S. Taylor was formerly one of the selectmen, and now holds the position of town treasurer. He is also chairman on building committee of the new school house. This firm are engaged in the manufacture of starch, but give particular attention to the sale of groceries and provisions, boots and shoes, dry goods, etc., and makes a specialty of lumbermen's and farmer's supplies, being prepared to fill the largest orders at short notice and furnish reliable goods at positively bottom rates.

C. B. ROBERTS,

Attorney at Law and Notary Public.

OFFICE IN ROBERTS' BLOCK. MAIN STREET,

CARIBOU, - MAINE.

HANSON & PILTZ, Groceries, Fish, etc., Caribou, Me.—Any one at all familiar with the grocery business would need no further evidence of the fact that Messrs. Hanson & Piltz cater especially to family trade, than that afforded by the character of the goods they handle, for their stock has been selected with great care, and is made up of just such articles as will give satisfaction to the most critical. It includes staple and fancy groceries of all kinds. This firm also make a specialty of fresh fish, keeping a full supply of all kinds constantly on hand, and the goods are offered at positively the lowest market rates, quality considered, and are fully warranted to prove just as represented. Under these circumstances it is not surprising that an extensive trade should already have been built up, although operations were not begun until 1891. The firm is constituted of Mr. Chas. P. Hanson, who is a native of Massachusetts, and served in the army during the Rebellion, and Mr. G. T. Piltz, a native of Sweden. Both partners give personal attention to customers and prompt and polite service is assured at all times.

McNELLY & McLELLAN, dealers in Men's, Boys' and Children's Ready-Made Clothing, Hats, Caps and Furnishing Goods, Trunks, Bags, Valises, etc., Sweden Street, Caribou, Me.—There are many able and enterprising merchants in Caribou and vicinity—men who know every detail of their business, know the trade they are catering to, and know just the sort of goods they prefer—but nowhere in town can a more skillfully chosen and more desirable stock of goods be found than at the establishment of Messrs. McNelly & McLellan, located on Sweden street. This concern is composed of Messrs. P. L. McNelly and William McLellan and began operations in 1889. The firm deal in men's, boys' and children's ready-made clothing, hats, caps, furnishing goods, trunks, bags, valises, etc., and both as regards the variety and quality of the goods and the prices quoted offer inducements very hard to equal and impossible to surpass elsewhere. A stylish, perfect-fitting, well-made and durable garment or suit may be bought here for very little money, and whether you buy a dress suit or a working suit, a hat or a necktie, in fact anything, you may depend on its proving just as represented and on getting full value for your money every time. Goods are cheerfully shown and prices quoted, all callers, whether they wish to buy or only to look around, being assured prompt attention and polite treatment.

D. E. JOHNSON, dealer in Furniture and Caskets. Undertaker's Supplies always on hand. Caribou, Me.—Mr. D. E. Johnson carries on the only furniture store in town, but even if there were a dozen others there is no doubt but that the one conducted by Mr. Johnson would be largely patronized, for the simple reason that he gives excellent value to customers, the inducements offered comparing very favorably with those held out by dealers doing business in the leading cities of the State. Coffins and caskets as well as furniture are dealt in and a full line of undertakers' supplies is constantly on hand, so that orders can be filled without delay. This business was founded many years ago by Messrs. York & Hussey, and was carried on by Mrs. Hussey who was succeeded in 1885 by Mr. T. W. Willis, he giving place in 1890 to the present proprietor, who is a native of Garland, Me., and has a very large circle of friends throughout this section. The premises utilized by Mr. Johnson are 28×30 feet in dimensions, exclusive of a commodious storehouse, so that opportunity is given for the carrying of a large stock, and this is so fully availed of that practically all orders can be filled without delay, moderate charges being made in every instance.

N. W. JOHNSON, dealer in Groceries, Corn, Flour, Tea, Coffee, Spice, etc., Caribou, Me.—The question of whether Caribou has become an important trade centre on account of the number and excellence of the stores here, or the number and excellence of the stores have made the town an important trade centre is something like the famous question, "Which was first, the hen or the egg?" and is of no great consequence anyway, the main point being that people can buy to better advantage here than elsewhere and therefore trade here more extensively every year. The store carried on by Mr. N. W. Johnson may be called a truly representative establishment for it has done much to extend Caribou's reputation as a place where excellent value may be obtained for money expended. Mr. Johnson is a native of Garland, Me., and has carried on his present store some eight or nine years. He deals in dry goods, groceries, corn, flour, tea, coffee, spices, boots and shoes, and other standard commodities, utilizing premises of the dimensions of 26×48 feet, and carrying a very large and well chosen stock. The goods are uniformly reliable, are sold at the lowest market rates, and callers are promptly and carefully attended to, so that the popularity of this establishment is thoroughly well deserved.

J. S. GETCHELL & SON,

CARIBOU, ME.,

Iron and Wood Workers,

are prepared to do all kinds of mill work and jobbing, also manufacture circular saw mills, shingle machines, clapboard planers, horse hoes, plows, etc., besides dealing in new and second-hand machinery, and have saws, belting and steam fittings always on hand. They also have a well equipped planing mill, where all kinds of wood work, such as planing, matching, turning, etc., is done. They have constantly on hand doors and windows with trimmings, mouldings, hard and soft wood (kiln dried) flooring and finish, and are prepared to furnish these in any quantity desired.

LUFKIN & HOLMES, Agents, Groceries and Dry Goods, Caribou, Me.—The establishment carried on by Messrs. Lufkin & Holmes occupies a leading position among the representative stores of this section of the State, and what is more it fully deserves its prominence and popularity for they are the results of years of honest, intelligent and able public service. The business was formerly carried on by Mr. H. H. Lufkin, and in 1885 he became associated with Mr. P. K. Holmes under the present firm-name. Mr. Lufkin is a native of Maine, and Mr. Holmes of New Brunswick. The former served in the army during the Rebellion, and has been one of the selectmen of this town; both he and Mr. Holmes being universally known and highly esteemed throughout this section. The firm utilize spacious premises and deal very largely in general merchandise, among the more important commodities handled being groceries, dry goods, fancy goods, hardware, boots and shoes, and paints and oils. Sewing machines must also be given special mention, they being agents for "The White," the most durable sewing machine in the market, and unsurpassed for general efficiency. Bottom prices rule at this popular establishment and all goods are sold strictly on their merits, no pains being spared to satisfy every customer, and another very popular feature is the care taken to give prompt and painstaking attention to every caller, and use every buyer so fairly that no reasonable cause for complaint can be shown.

E. E. DOUGLAS, Shingle Mill, Caribou, Me.—The question of what is the best material with which to cover a roof has engaged the attention of architects and builders for centuries, and although almost innumerable materials and forms of the same material have been tried nothing has as yet been found that can compare with shingles as regards the combination of lightness, efficiency, durability, cheapness, ornamental appearance, and ease of repairing which distinguishes them from all others and has caused them to be used on four-fifths of the roofs in this country. Maine furnishes a large proportion of the shingles used in New England, and this portion of the State furnishes a large share of the Maine production, there being many shingle mills hereabouts, and among them that carried on by Mr. E. E. Douglas, who is a native of Trenton, Me., and began operations here in 1889. His mill is fitted up with improved machinery, and he is prepared to fill orders promptly and to furnish shingles accurately graded and of standard quality at the lowest market rates. Employment is given to five assistants.

H. G. HAYDEN & CO., dealers in Meats, Groceries, Provisions, etc., Caribou, Me.—It is safe to assume that there is not one of our readers but what has had more or less difficulty in getting meats to suit him (or her, and it is generally "her," for the ladies do the most of the marketing), for there is no other commodity so variable in quality and hard to select accurately, even those who make a business of handling it being often deceived by its appearance. But, of course, an experienced dealer can generally judge pretty accurately and that is one reason why we should advise those wishing first class meats to place their orders with Messrs. H. G. Hayden & Co., for this concern make a specialty of handling such, and can satisfy the most critical tastes, they sparing no pains to provide just the quality asked for by the customer. Another reason for recommending this house is that they carry a large and varied stock, including not only fresh, salted, corned and smoked meats but also groceries of every description, eggs, butter and country produce in general. The prices are right, too, and in short the service offered is exceptionally satisfactory in every department, as is shown by the wide popularity of the enterprise. It was formerly carried on by Messrs. J. A. Morrill & Co., who were succeeded by Messrs. Hayden & Small, the present firm-name being adopted in 1891. Employment is given to two assistants, and callers are assured prompt and careful attention.

MISS L. F. RUNNALS, Books and Stationery, Caribou, Me.—The people of the United States have been called a "nation of readers," and the name is most appropriate, for the love of reading is confined to no particular class here but is common to rich and poor and is especially prominent in that great "middle class," as social students call it, which here as elsewhere is by far the most valuable as it is by far the largest portion of the community. Hence the popularity of the store carried on by Miss L. F. Runnals is not at all difficult to account for, as one may always find here a skillfully chosen assortment of books, including the latest novels, etc., and the prices quoted are low as the lowest. Stationery is also dealt in, together with writing materials of all kinds, the stock being very complete and including many late and attractive novelties in the line of fashionable papers, envelopes, etc., as well as a full assortment of stationery for business use. Miss Runnals is a native of Garland, Me., and has been identified with her present enterprise since 1889.

ALL WORK FIRST-CLASS.

F. S. SMITH, PORTRAIT PHOTOGRAPHER,

ROBERTS' BLOCK, CARIBOU, MAINE.

Instantaneous Process used Exclusively in our Studio.

Life size crayons a specialty and at prices within the reach of all.   Copies or enlargements from old pictures at reasonable rates.   Views of every description made to order and all negatives preserved.   Pictures of all kinds framed to order.

ALBEE HOLMES, manufacturer of Shingles and Starch, Caribou, Me.—It being an obvious fact that that country is most prosperous whose natural resources are most perfectly developed, it follows that those most actively engaged in developing the resources of a given section are to be given a large share of the credit for whatever degree of prosperity that section may enjoy, and hence Mr. Albee Holmes must be accorded a prominent position among the representative business men of this county, he being largely engaged in the manufacture of two of its principal products, shingles and starch.   He is thoroughly familiar with the details of each branch of production, and as he controls extensive and improved facilities he is in a position to fill the largest orders at short notice, and also to meet all honorable competition by quoting positively the lowest market rates on articles of standard and guaranteed merit.

MRS. R. A. BARTLETT, Millinery and Fancy Goods, Caribou, Me.—There is a popular conviction that "what everybody says must be true," and, as "everybody" says that the establishment carried on by Mrs. R. A. Bartlett is surpassed by no other in this section of the State devoted to the same line of business, it certainly well deserves prominent mention in these pages.   This business was founded about eighteen years ago, and as it has been ably and successfully conducted from the first, it is not to be wondered at that it should be universally known and highly popular.   Mrs. Bartlett deals in millinery and fancy goods of all kinds, and carries a very carefully chosen stock including the very latest fashionable novelties in hats, bonnets and trimmings of every description.   Particular attention is given to custom work, and results are attained such as are possible only when good taste is combined with long and varied experience and excellent facilities.   Employment is given to five assistants during the busy season, and orders can therefore be filled at short notice, no pains being spared to deliver goods promptly at the time agreed upon, and no inferior work being knowingly allowed to leave the establishment, Mrs. Bartlett giving personal supervision to the filling of every order.

E. H. PUSHOR, manufacturer of Dr. Flick's Scratch Ointment, and Druggist, Caribou, Me.—So long as drugs and medicines are used in the treatment of disease a well stocked and well managed drug store will be one of the most valuable establishments a community can have, and certainly none of our Caribou readers will deny that the drug store carried on by Mr. E. H Pushor is as useful and popular an establishment as can be found in town.   Mr. Pushor is a native of Pittsfield, Me , and has conducted his present store about ten years, having begun operations in 1881.   He deals in books, stationery, fancy articles, etc., offering a large and desirable assortment and quoting low prices, but he makes a leading specialty of

drugs, medicines and chemicals, and constantly carries a large and very complete stock selected from the most reliable sources.   Prescriptions will be accurately and promptly compounded, and no unreasonable charges are made, the prices quoted comparing favorably with those-named in the leading city pharmacies.   Mr. Pushor is the manufacturer of Dr. Flick's Scratch Ointment, and sells it all over the country, for it is known and prized in all parts of the Union, and its popularity and celebrity are especially remarkable from the fact that they have not been aided by extensive advertising, but have been brought about by the superior merits of the ointment, it being conceded to have no equal in its special line.

D. M. MOODY, manufacturer of all Kinds of Carriages and Heavy Wagons, Caribou, Me.—If ever a process be devised by which first-class carriages or wagons may be made out of second-class material it will then be possible to get a first-class vehicle at a second class price, but under present conditions those who try to do so will "get left" every time.   But although a first-class vehicle commands a first-class price it is not necessary to pay a fancy price for one and those who do so really pay two prices—one for the vehicle and one for the "name" of the maker.   Mr. D. M. Moody manufactures as good carriages and heavy wagons as can be found in the market, and he has the reputation of doing so, too, but he does not charge extra for the reputation, and so you can get a thoroughly satisfactory vehicle from him at a price considerably lower than is usually quoted on one of equal excellence made elsewhere.   Mr. Moody is a native of Thorndike, Me., and began operations in Caribou in 1882.   His shop has two floors, each 35×90 feet in size, and there are two one story wings each measuring 12×35 feet.   The premises contain a complete plant of improved machinery, driven by a ten horse power engine, and employment is given to ten assistants, so that custom work, repairing, etc., can be done at very short notice.   Carefully selected materials are used, every process incidental to production is skillfully carried out, and the result is that work from this shop looks well and wears well; giving uniform satisfaction and proving the cheapest as well as the best in the long run.

VAUGHAN HOUSE, B. J. Smith, Proprietor. Hack to and from all trains. Caribou, Me.—It is said there is more traveling done in the United States in pro portion to population than in any other country in the world, and as hotels are supported almost entirely by the traveling public it is not surprising that our hotels out number and outclass those of any other nation. Of course there are many poor hotels in this country as well as many good ones but the proportion of inferior public houses is steadily diminishing, and this is due, in a great measure, to the fact that a really good hotel is the most profitable in the long run, as its patrons increase its trade by constantly recommending it. In our opinion this is a duty which every traveler owes to the public in general, and hence we take pleasure in recommending the Vaughan House and feel confident that our recommendation will be endorsed by all who may make trial of the accommodations there offered, for the hotel is commodious and well arranged, is comfortably furnished, well heated, well ventilated, well lighted and well managed. The proprietor, Mr. B. J. Smith is a native of Hodgdon, Me., and was in the army during the Rebellion. He has been identified with the Vaughan House since 1884, and from the first has spared no pains to promote the comfort of guests and to carry on a hotel that should deserve hearty and continuous support. There are thirty-five sleeping-rooms in the house, which is lit by electricity and fully equipped in every respect. The table is supplied with an abundant variety of seasonable food, and as twelve assistants are employed the service is prompt and efficient at all times. Hacks are run to and from all trains, and there is a first class livery, board and feed stable, containing thirty stalls, connected with the hotel and affording excellent accommodations at reasonable rates.

MRS. N. M. LOWNEY, Fruit and Confectionery, Sweden Street, Caribou, Me.—The figures show that the consumption of fruit in this country is steadily and rapidly increasing, and this is certainly a good thing for the public, for fruit is known to be the most healthful of foods, and when in good condition it will do more to keep one in health than any drug or medicine possibly could. It is easy to get fruit of good quality by going to the right place, and you cannot do better than to patronize the store of which Mrs. N. M. Lowney is owner, for she takes care to get the best the market affords, and her assortment is varied and her prices reasonable. Confectionery is also dealt in, pure candies of fine flavor being always in stock, and during the summer months ice-cream is a prominent specialty, and it is generally conceded that the cream here sold is unequalled for uniform delicacy of flavor. Mrs. Lowney is a native of Presque Isle, Me., began business in 1890, and has built up a good and steadily growing trade, her store being favorably known throughout this vicinity.

HISTORICAL SKETCH OF PRESQUE ISLE.

Presque Isle is the southernmost of those three remarkable towns which lie adjacent to one another and whose principal villages are so located that straight lines drawn from one to the other would form a triangle having very nearly equal sides and with the apex inclined towards the north-west. Each township is double the ordinary size, it having an area of 72 square miles ; each includes some of the most fertile land in the country ; each has valuable water powers, railway facilities, and an industrious and energetic population ; and as it is an axiom that "like causes produce like effects" it is not surprising that these three towns — Presque Isle, Fort Fairfield and Caribou — should strongly resemble one another in rapidity of growth, past advancement and future prospects. In fact they may not inaptly be called "the Aroostook triplets," for they were born (or in other words incorporated) at about the same time, they draw their nourishment from the same sources, and in many respects have a strong "family" resemblance although each has its own individual characteristics. They are magnificently strong and healthy infants (for infants they are although more than thirty years have passed since their incorporation, a third of a century being but a short period in the life of a town), and like all sturdy children they delight in generous emulation and like to "stump" one another to perform difficult feats, but the rivalry is as good-natured as it is keen, and each town knows full well it could safely depend upon the others in time of serious trouble. Each is destined to become a city, probably before it enters upon its second half-century of existence, and each gives promise of immense development in the immediate future, the natural resources of the adjacent country being practically inexhaustible and the outlook from an agricultural, from a manufacturing and from a mercantile point of view being favorable in the highest degree. The similarity of these towns in age and in present importance may be appreciated by an examination of the following figures :

	Incorporated.	Population 1890.			Valuation 1890.
Presque Isle,	April 4, 1859,	3046	Polls, 672 ; estates,	$993,875.00	
Fort Fairfield,	March 11, 1858,	3526	" 747 "	893,593.00	
Caribou,	April 5, 1859,	4087	" 876 "	780,439.00	

The aggregate population is 10,659 and the aggregate valuation of estates is $2,667,907.00 ; the average population being 3,553 and the average estate valuation $889,302.00. It is worthy of note that Presque Isle combines the smallest population with the largest valuation, while an exactly opposite condition of affairs prevails at Caribou, that town having the largest population and the smallest valuation. But on the whole, the three towns are very equally matched and although the above figures represent the condition of affairs in 1890 and do not give an adequate idea of the present population and wealth of these three rapidly growing communities, they enable intelligent comparison of them to be made, for the progress made by the three towns since that date has been substantially equal, so that no change in their comparative positions has occurred.

When Presque Isle was incorporated, in 1859, the township was but one-half its present size, and its importance in other respects may be estimated from the census figures of the following year, the population in 1860 being 723, the polls 161 and the valuation of estates $79,874.00. Comparatively slight gain was made during the succeeding decade, the population in 1870 having been 970, the number of polls 182, and the valuation of estates $180,726.00, but during the ten years from 1870 to 1880 development proceeded more rapidly and the result was that in 1880 the population had increased to 1305, the number of polls to 295 and the valuation of estates to $339,325.00. But this growth was as nothing compared with the development from 1880 to 1890, for during this period of time the population increased nearly three hundred per cent, the population increasing from 1,305 to 3,046, the number of polls from 295 to 672 and the valuation of estates from $339,325.00 to $993,-875.00. This enormous growth, however, was largely due to the doubling of the area of the township by the annexation of Maysville, which adjoined it on the north and which became a part of Presque Isle February 14, 1883. Maysville was incorporated the same day that Presque Isle was, April 4, 1859, and in 1880 had a population of 1,141, and its estates were valued at $224,288.00. It was a famous farming town and at the time of annexation contained a large starch factory and several saw mills. Presque Isle village was always the centre of business for Maysville so that the interests of the two

BIRD'S EYE VIEW OF PRESQUE ISLE.

towns were in many respects identical even before they were legally combined by annexation. The residents of Maysville took justifiable pride in the excellence of the town's roads and about 500 shade trees were set out along the highways in a single year. The name Maysville is still borne by the northern half of the township of Presque Isle and as the two sections differ considerably in topography it is better to treat of each of them separately in preparing a description of the town, first stating, however, that the township as a whole is bounded on the north by Caribou, on the east by Fort Fairfield and Easton, on the south by Westfield plantation and on the west by Chapman, Mapleton and Washburn. It lies in the second range of Aroostook county townships, and Presque Isle village would occupy just about the middle of a straight line drawn from Houlton to the northern limits of the county, it being about forty miles, in an air line, from either point, and forty-two miles north northwest of Houlton by the stage line running from that town to Caribou. It is situated on Presque Isle stream, very near what was once the Maysville line and a little to the west of the centre of the township. The middle of the original Presque Isle township is generally elevated, and south by south-west of the village is Green Mountain, having four peaks and lying in a true north and south line. A little to the west of the middle line of the town in its southern part is Quaggy Joe Lake, which is one mile long and is drained by Arnold Brook. Presque Isle stream enters the town from the west and takes a northeasterly course to the village, thence flowing north and emptying into the Aroostook River about midway of its course through Maysville. The stream furnishes good water power at the village and has been utilized for manufacturing purposes from an early period in the town's history.

The manufacturing interests of the town are quite extensive also, there being valuable water powers at the village and considerable steam power being utilized. There are mills at Spragueville, near Quaggy Joe Lake, as well as at Presque Isle village and elsewhere, and the more important productions of the town include long and short lumber, starch, woodwork of various kinds such as doors, sash, mouldings, etc., cabinet work, brick, carriages, harness, coffins and caskets, meal and feed, machine work, marble work, axes, general blacksmiths' work, hides and leather, tin-work, etc. Wool carding is also done and there are many minor manufactures, as for instance, those carried on by tailors, dressmakers, milliners, printers, photographers, etc.

RESIDENCE OF A. M. SMITH.

The commercial interests of Presque Isle village are varied and important for, as we have previously stated, this village has been the trade center for all the country adjacent from the very first. Numerous fine business blocks, large and elegant stores, and heavy and varied stocks attest the prosperity and enterprise of the local merchants, and it is a frequent saying among the people that an article of merchandise that cannot be found at Presque Isle cannot be found anywhere in the county. In the stocks of local merchants may be found anything from diamonds to telegraph poles and from watches to mowing machines; while the assortments of clothing, of furnishings, of jewelry and of other goods whose design is influenced by the caprices of fashion are so complete and embrace so many of the very latest novelties that visiting strangers from Bangor, from Portland, from Boston or from other great trade centres are generally more surprised by these stocks than by any other thing they see in this, to them, wonderful country, for they find that they can buy here (within reasonable limitations) to as good advantage as they could at home, and it is a constant marvel to them that the tradesmen of so remote a town as this appears to them to be can sell so cheaply and offer so great and desirable a variety to choose from.

The handsome and modern appearance of the business edifices in the village is largely due to what so often proves to be a blessing although it is never welcomed as such,—an extensive conflagration. In 1886 the business portion of the village was almost totally destroyed by fire so that practically none of the present mercantile structures are more than five years old at the farthest. But "purification by fire," although thoroughly effectual, is too expensive and entails too much danger and inconvenience to be practiced as a regular thing, and therefore as soon as affairs had been straightened out a little after the conflagration the residents of the town took steps to prevent the fire king from again becoming unduly familiar should he re-visit the town by making arrangements to give him a cool and moist reception on the instant of his arrival. The Presque Isle Water Company was formed in 1887 with George H. Freeman, M.D., as president and superintendent, and the company went actively to work to bring into the village an abundant supply of water that should be as pure and wholsome as it was effectual in subduing an incipient blaze. Competent engineering advice was sought, a compre-hensive and efficient plan decided upon, and the result is that Presque Isle now has a water supply

copious enough to satisfy the most ardent prohibitionist and reliable enough to reassure the most timid citizen when he lies awake o' nights and figures out how largely his destructible. property exceeds the amount of his insurance policies. The water is taken from Kennedy Brook, which drains a watershed having an area of about twenty-eight square miles and which is copiously fed by springs so that the water is singularly pure and clear, and as regards both quality and quantity is all that could be desired. The reservoir has a capacity of 35,000,000 gallons and is located 100 feet above Main street, the pressure resulting from this elevation being about forty pounds. A Worthington steam pump of sufficient capacity to provide for all probable needs for years to come is an important feature of the plant, the entire expense of which was $30,000.

Another first-class plant utilized for public purposes is that operated by the Presque Isle Electric Light Company, of which Mr. Sidney Graves is superintendent. The Edison incandescent system is used and gives entire satisfaction to consumers as well as to the company,— which is certainly all that can be expected from any "system," electric or otherwise. The superintendent of the electric light company occupies another important official position also, he being chief engineer of the fire depart-ment, which is completely equipped, efficiently organized and is fully capable of handling any fire which is at all liable to occur in the village.

A town which has a first-class water supply ought not to allow itself to get along without an efficient system of sewerage, and the residents of Presque Isle are evidently of this opinion, for a com-prehensive system of drainage has been inaugurated and its details are being extended every year. Presque Isle is a healthful town and proposes to remain so if intelligently devised and impartially enforced hygienic measures can ensure the maintenance of the present condition of affairs, for there is an active· and efficient board of health, made up of Messrs. C. P. Allen, F. Kilburne, and C. F. Daggett.

The spiritual needs of the people are as well looked after as are the physical needs, there being six handsome church buildings in the village, each of which is owned by the society worshiping therein, and the religious societies include associations of Baptists, Free Baptists, Episcopals, Congregationalists, Unitarians, Methodists and Christians. Churches and schools are intimately related, in New England communities at least, and therefore it is natural that a town having the excellent church facilities possessed by Presque Isle should control first-class educational facilities also. Not only is the public school system comprehensive, well conducted, and very generally availed of, but it is most admirably supplemented by the work of St. John's English and Classical School, of which Mr. W. T. Elmer is principal. The premises utilized by this institution are extensive, the buildings well arranged and well equipped, and the course of study practical and very thoroughly carried out, the school having a high reputation and being by no means an unimportant factor in the promotion of the interests of the town. The fraternal associations of Presque Isle are many and prosperous, among them being a Masonic lodge; several associations of Odd Fellows; a lodge of Knights of Pythias; two societies of Patrons of Husbandry; G. A. R. Post L. B. Wade, No. 123; Relief Corps; Sons of Veterans; Women's Christian Temperance Union; Good Templars; besides other associations not of a fraternal character, such as the Presque Isle Band and Palmer's Orchestra. The town has excellent banking facilities, furnished by local institutions, and it also has first-class hotel accommodations, the local public houses being large and well-kept. Of course so wide-awake a community supports a local newspaper, and as a matter of fact it supports two of them both weeklies; the *Aroostook Democrat* being published Thursdays, by Mr. George H. Collins, and the *Star-Herald* being published Wednesdays, by the Aroostook Democrat Publishing Company. Both the great political parties are represented and both papers devote a large amount of space to local news besides containing a great deal of matter of general interest. Their advertising columns are well patronized and both publications are skillfully edited and ably represent the enterprising town and section in which they are located. The industrial and mercantile interests of Presque Isle are also carefully looked after by the local Board of Trade, of which George H. Freeman is president, George H. Collins is secretary, and J. W. Bolton is treasurer. This organization makes a specialty of furnishing dependable and "inside" information to out-of-town parties investigating the business chances offered within the township, and all communications addressed to the secretary will receive prompt and careful attention. There are many and valuable opportunities now open at Presque Isle to men with capital, energy and ability; the building of the Bangor and Aroostook railroad will enlarge these opportunities to an almost unlimited extent, and in this connection the following quotation from one of Maine's many energetic newspapers will prove of interest and will furnish a most appropriate ending to this sketch of one of her most promising towns.

"Maine is certainly in the line of development and increase in wealth and population. Capital is beginning to flow into this State, and the magnificent water powers of the Pine Tree State are beginning to be utilized by many different kinds of manufactures.

"The drift of manufactures, fully as much as that of summer travel, is now Maineward, and both mean more railroads, more wealth, more people, and a much more important position for the State in years to come than she has had in years past. Fifteen years ago who would have dared predict that summer visitors would flock hither and sow millions of dollars yearly over the length and breadth of this rugged old State? But they do, and Maine people know how to make a good use of these dollars that slip from the easy and careless fingers of millionaires.

"Who would have predicted that every few weeks a party of capitalists would be exploring Maine for the best site for some immense manufacturing plant, involving the investment of hundreds of thousands of dollars and the employment of hundreds of hands?

"All these things show that Maine's turn has come. There is the elastic force of a general boom in prosperity under every Maine enterprise now in contemplation, and that is going to help boost the Aroostook railroad, almost as much as the great inducements the County itself offers to the building of a road. The road is sure to come, not only because Aroostook is big and productive and full of immense undeveloped resources, but because Maine is a coming State, and enterprise and business activity are the rule all along the line."— *North Star.*

Representative Business Men of Presque Isle, Me.

A. M. SMITH & CO., dealers in Hardware, Tinware, Stoves and Furnaces, Lamps, Glassware, etc., Presque Isle, Me.—The store of which Messrs. A. M. Smith & Co. are the proprietors is one of those establishments at which one is always sure to find desirable goods, and at which bottom prices are quoted, so that it is not at all surprising that it should be one of the most popular in town. The business was founded by Mr. A. M. Smith about 1880, and in 1883 he became associated with Mr. E. W. Fernald, under the existing firm name. Both partners are natives of Maine, and both are very widely known throughout this section, especially Mr. Smith, who holds the position of town treasurer. The concern deal in hardware, tinware, stoves, furnaces, lamps, glassware, kitchen furnishings, etc., and carry a large and desirable stock, the premises utilized having an area of about 7,000 square feet. The productions of the leading manufacturers are handled, and the agricultural tools, stoves, lamps and other goods offered by this enterprising firm embody the latest improvements, are first-class in material and workmanship, and, although sold at bottom figures, are guaranteed to prove just as represented in every respect.

THE PEOPLE'S CASH STORE, D. H. Ervin, dealer in Dry and Fancy Goods, Hosiery, Gloves and Corsets, Ladies' and Gents' Furnishing Goods, Hats Caps, Boots, Shoes and Rubbers. Samples of Dress Goods mailed on application. No. 13 Union Block, Presque Isle, Me.—We have no fear but what the ladies of Presque Isle and vicinity will agree with us when we say that no "shopping" tour is looked upon as complete unless it includes the establishment conducted by Mr. D. H. Ervin, of "The People's Cash Store," at No. 13 Union Block, in this town, for this store is in some respects unique and always offers many attractions impossible to find elsewhere, and then again, these inducements are constantly varying ; because you have visited the store Monday is no reason why you cannot profitably visit it again Tuesday or Wednesday, for the stock is constantly being renewed, fresh novelties being added at such frequent intervals that the only way to "keep up with the times," so far as this popular store is concerned, is to visit it early and often. The present proprietor, who is a native of Nova Scotia, assumed control in 1890, and is generally well known in this vicinity. He gives close attention to the supervision of affairs and spares no pains to maintain the enviable reputation long associated with this enterprise. Mr. Ervin is an extensive retail dealer in dry and fancy goods ladies' ready-made garments of all kinds, hosiery, gloves and corsets, ladies' and gents' furnishing goods, hats, caps, boots, shoes and rubbers, and is prepared to quote the lowest market rates on large or small orders. The stock is varied and complete and made up of articles that can safely be guaranteed.

T. N. ERVIN, dealer in Groceries and Provisions, Dry Goods, Boots and Shoes, Hats, Caps, etc., No. 15 Main Street, Presque Isle, Me.—The flourishing business conducted by Mr. T. N. Ervin, was founded by him in 1880. He is a native of Nova Scotia, and very widely and favorably known in this vicinity. The premises owned by this enterprising and reliable merchant are located on Main street and comprise two stores, one of which measures 26×60 and the other 22×60 feet ; also a store-house 25×40 feet. The establishment is throughout admirably adapted to the display of merchandise, the convenience of customers and the dispatch of business. The stock is most extensive and consists of groceries and provisions, dry goods, boots and shoes, hats, caps, etc. Every thing in this wide range of merchandise is supplied at lowest prices and goods are warranted satisfactory, and full confidence is universally inspired by the business methods and worth of this representative dealer. Both a wholesale and retail trade is done, the extent of which necessitates the employment of three competent clerks and orders are promptly filled and goods dispatched at short notice, and the prices on all are uniformly low. Courteous attention is given to callers at all times. Goods are delivered to all parts of the village free of charge.

H. L. & F. A. LEONARD, dealers in Fresh and Salt Meats, Fish, Provisions, Groceries and Canned Goods, Spices, Teas and Tobacco, Presque Isle, Me.—Although the advantages of housekeeping far outweigh its disadvantages, it must be confessed that the trials and disappointments of the average housekeeper are many, and that the larger portion of them are connected with the obtaining of food supplies, for it is at times very difficult to obtain food, and especially meats, that will prove altogether satisfactory. This is by no means entirely the fault of the dealer, but nevertheless a great saving of time, money and patience may be made by trading with a reputable and well equipped house, and hence we feel that we are doing some of our readers a service by calling to their attention the facilities possessed by Messrs. H. L. & F. A. Leonard for furnishing meats, fish, provisions and groceries of standard quality at the lowest market rates. The store occupied is centrally located, and is 30×50 feet in dimensions, being sufficiently roomy to accommodate the large stock mentioned above, the assortment, which also includes canned goods, teas, spices and tobacco, being so varied that all tastes and purses can be suited. In connection a slaughter house is located about one mile out of Presque Isle, supplying fresh meats at all seasons. Messrs. Leonard are both natives of this State, and became identified with their present enterprise in 1885, and have attained a high reputation as enterprising and honorable merchants.

ESTABLISHED 1884.

ST. JOHN'S SCHOOL,

PRESQUE ISLE, ME.

Rt. Rev. HENRY A. NEELY, D.D., Visitor.　　　Rev. WM. T. ELMER, Principal.

Th s school gives a thorough preparation for college or scientific school, the study of any profession, or for business life.

The buildings are new, spacious and well appointed, and the grounds ample for all field exercises.

Twenty-five boys will be received as boarders in the house of the Principal.

A chapel, gymnasium, drill hall — U. S. rifles, and a chemical and philosophical laboratory form part of the equipment of the school. No pains are spared to make the school a comfortable and refined home for boys.

For further information apply to the Principal.

HONE BROTHERS, dealers in Groceries and Provisions, Crockery and Glassware, Tobacco, Fruits and Canned Goods of all Kinds, Presque Isle, Me.—It is always a good idea to trade with an enterprising house whenever such a course is possible for the customers of a wide awake and progressive concern are sure to be treated with liberality and are also sure to receive their share of any increase in the concern's prosperity. The latter statement may be disputed by some people who pride themselves on their shrewdness and who will say that no firm is going to give its customers anything more than it has to. But all the same we know it to be true, and we also know that the really successful business men, are not those who keep every advantage to themselves, but rather those who share with customers and thus largely increase their trade and income, although they may lesson the percentage of their profits. The enterprise conducted by Messrs. Hone Bros., in this town, is a good example to mention in this connection, and we hold that this firm is in a better position to-day, than they would have been had they pursued the short sighted policy too common in their business. This undertaking was started in 1887, and the premises in use, comprise a store 24×40 feet in dimensions. A large stock is carried including choice groceries and provisions, crockery and glassware, tobacco, fruits and canned goods of all kinds, and a large retail trade is done, every facility being at hand to fill all orders received with promptness and care.

L. S. JUDD & SON, dealers in Dry Goods and Carpets, Boots, Shoes, etc., etc., Presque Isle, Me.— No more truly representative establishment can be found in Presque Isle, than that carried on by Messrs. L. S. Judd & Son, for this enterprise was inaugurated very nearly a quarter of a century ago; and has since been conducted in a manner which has given it the leading position among similar undertakings in this section. This business was founded in 1860, by Messrs. Johnson & Judd, and after two changes in the firm name, came under the management of the present proprietors in 1871, composed of L. S. Judd and J. H. Judd, both natives of Connecticut. The premises occupied on Main street, are 25×60 feet in dimensions and a heavy and varied stock is carried consisting of dry goods and carpets, boots, shoes, etc., etc. We need hardly say that so old established and reputable a concern as this, is widely and favorably known among manufacturers and wholesalers, and hence is in a position to buy to the best advantage at the lowest market rates, and to offer special inducements to its customers. Nor is it necessary to dwell upon the fact that all articles bought here will prove as represented. The Presque Isle public have long since learned that "full value for money received," is the cardinal principle of the management, and the present magnitude of the business shows that this policy is not only known, but appreciated. Mr. L. S. Judd has been town clerk for twenty-one years and selectman twenty years.

T. H. PHAIR, manufacturer of Potato Starch and Lumber, Presque Isle, Me.; Mills at Presque Isle, Maysville, Washburn, Mapleton, Easton and Perham.— It would be very difficult to overestimate the importance of the great business carried on by Mr. T. H. Phair, that is, its importance so far as the residents of this section of the country are concerned, at all events, for not only does it afford remunerative employment to many directly but to many more indirectly, and it supplies a reliable means of disposing of immense quantities of one of the most staple and famous products of this portion of Maine— potatoes, for Mr. Phair is the largest manufacturer of potato starch in the world, carries on eight factories, produces from 1,000 to 2,000 tons annually, and pays out from $75,000 to $125,000 every year for potatoes alone, to say nothing of the wages of the 200 assistants that are employed in starch making two and one-half months in the year. The mills are located at Presque Isle, Maysville, Washburn, Mapleton, Easton and Perham. Mr. Phair is largely engaged in the manufacture of lumber, also, his lumber mills being located at Washburn, and this department of the business giving employment to fifty hands throughout the year. He is a native of New York and has had sole control of the enterprise under consideration since 1877, they having resulted from operations begun by Messrs. Johnson & Phair in 1865. The vast business is very thoroughly systemized, and orders are filled with a promptness and accuracy which might profitably be imitated by the management of many much smaller undertakings

H. B. THAYER, Druggist and Apothecary, and dealer in Stationery and Fancy Goods, No. 9 Union Block, Main Street, Presque Isle, Maine.—It is safe to say that no establishment in Presque Isle is more deserving of hearty and generous patronage than that conducted by Mr. H. B. Thayer, for no undertaking is of more genuine utility or more liberally managed. Mr. Thayer is a native of Garland, Maine, and has carried on his present business since 1885. He is a druggist and apothecary, and carries a complete stock of pure drugs, medicines and chemicals, obtaining them from the most reliable sources, and sparing no pains to handle as high a grade of goods as the market affords. Especial attention is given to the compounding of physicians' prescriptions, every facility being provided to ensure absolute accuracy in the smallest details of the work, and to enable orders to be filled at very short notice. Mr. Thayer also carries a complete assortment of stationery and fancy goods. The premises made use of comprise one store, 18×60 feet in dimensions, and contain, besides the articles already mentioned, a full line of stationery and fancy goods. Mr. Thayer's store is at No. 9 Union block, Main street, and he is prepared to furnish all the goods handled at bottom prices, and as one competent assistant is employed, all orders are assured immediate and careful attention.

PRESQUE ISLE CLOTHING COMPANY,

DEALERS IN ALL KINDS OF

READY-MADE CLOTHING,

HATS, CAPS, BOOTS,

SHOES AND RUBBERS.

In fact everything that a man would need to dress and make himself comfortable.

We are selling goods cheaper than they have ever been sold in Aroostook county.   Call and look our goods over and be convinced of the fact.

CHARLES A. BARTO, Manager.

B. B. GLIDDEN, dealer in all kinds of Furniture, Coffins, Caskets and Undertakers' Supplies ; Agent for New Home Sewing Machine ; Bridge Street, Presque Isle, Me.—The business conducted by Mr. B. B. Glidden on Bridge street, is one of the best managed of its kind in Presque Isle. Operations were begun here many years ago by F. A. Soule, but the present proprietor only took the management in 1884. He is a native of Sebec, Me., and is one of our most highly esteemed resident business men. The premises made use of comprise two floors 18×40 and 30×50 feet in dimensions. Mr. Glidden is a dealer in all kinds of furniture, coffins, caskets and undertakers' supplies, he carrying a large stock and being in a position to fill orders at very short notice, and the stock in hand is so arranged as to make examinations very easy. Coffins, caskets, etc., will be supplied at very moderate rates, and the assortment is sufficiently varied to allow all tastes and circumstances to be suited, Mr. Glidden being a manufacturer of coffins and caskets. An assistant is employed who is thoroughly experienced and reliable, and all commissions will be promptly, faithfully and intelligently executed.

M. C. SMITH, dealer in Flour and Groceries, Bridge Street, Presque Isle, Me.—It would be very difficult to find a more popular grocery store than that carried on by Mr. M. C. Smith on Bridge street, and those who argue that popularity is the result of "good luck," would do well to investigate the causes of the favor in which this establishment is held, for "luck" has had little or nothing to do with it, it having been brought about by hard, intelligent and prominent work, and a consistent policy of giving full value for all money received. The undertaking was founded several years ago by Mr. G. K. Nuttall, the present proprietor assuming control in 1888. He is a native of New Brunswick, and has had long experience in the grocery business, so that the close personal supervision he gives to the details of his present enterprise is a powerful factor in assuring its continued success. The premises occupied comprise a store 25×50 feet in dimensions, together with a storehouse, so that a large stock of choice flour and groceries is constantly carried and dealt in, and the lowest market rates are quoted on goods of standard merit. Employment is given to competent assistants, and if every caller does not receive prompt and courteous attention it is no fault of the management, for the rule is equal service to all, large or small, young or old, rich or poor, business being conducted so far as is possible on the "first come, first served" principle.

"THE BOUQUET," Smith & Barto, Millinery and Fancy Goods, 26 Main Street, Presque Isle, Me.—It is not difficult to ascertain that the establishment known as "The Bouquet," conducted by Smith & Barto, at No. 26 Main street, is a favorite resort with the ladies of Presque Isle and vicinity, for those who have had dealings at the store in question are outspoken in their commendation of the methods of the management pursued here. It is generally understood that the stock of millinery, fancy goods, etc., is one of the most carefully selected in the town, and also that the goods contained therein can be strictly depended upon to prove just as represented. This enterprise was inaugurated in 1886, and has met with steadily increasing patronage as its merits became more evident. The premises occupied cover an area of 1600 feet, and afford ample room to display the various articles carried in stock to excellent advantage. The firm is composed of Miss Laila E. Smith and Miss Clara E. Barto, both natives of this State, well and favorably known in this community. Fine millinery goods, comprising ribbons, laces, velvets, flowers, feathers, etc., are to be found in great variety at this establishment, and the prices satisfactory.

F. GOODHUE, dealer in Crockery and Glass, Silver Ware, Lamp Goods, Wall Paper, Curtains, etc., Presque Isle, Me.—A tasteful dinner set or tea set adds so much to the enjoyment of a meal and to the appearance of a table, that it may justly be classed high among the things which make a home attractive, and beautiful sets can now be bought for so small an amount of money, that there is no reason why all should not possess them. Should any of our readers doubt this statement, we will not waste their time and our own in argument, but will simply advise them to visit the establishment conducted by Mr. F. Goodhue, for here may be found the latest novelties in crockery and glass ware, besides a full stock of silver ware, lamp goods, wall paper, curtains, etc. The lowest market rates are quoted on all the goods handled. The store used is located centrally in Bolton's new block, City square, and measures 20×45 feet with basement. The stock is fresh, varied and attractive, the articles composing it are guaranteed to prove as represented and prompt and polite attention is assured to every caller. Mr. Goodhue is a native of Albion, Me., and has carried on his present enterprise since 1879, the firm name at that time being Goodhue & Lane, they being succeeded in 1890 by the present proprietor who has built up a large business by enterprising methods and fair dealing, and those who have dealt with him, will agree with us in all we say.

WHEN in PRESQUE ISLE, and in want of strictly

FINE GROCERIES,

drop into

FRED. BARKER'S,

where you will receive prompt attention and a kindly welcome.

JOSEPH I. ROBERTS, Planing and Moulding Mill, Presque Isle.—It is said that American wood work-ing machinery is the most efficient in the world, and it is easy to believe that such is the case, for it would seem impossible to further improve on some of the machinery found in our moulding, planing and saw mills. The mill carried on by Mr. Joseph Roberts is a good place to observe to what perfection wood-working machinery has been brought, for it is very completely fitted up, and a large variety of work, including turning, planing, mould-ing, and band sawing is done here in accordance with the most approved methods. Mr. Roberts is a native of Caribou, Maine, and succeeded Mr. W. D. Graves, Jr., in 1890. He gives close attention to the filling of orders, and is moderate in his charges, although his work is unsur-passed for accuracy, and commissions are execute l at very short notice, the mill comprising two floors, 30×75 feet in size, and ample water power being available.

JOHN WILSON & SON, Manufacturers of Builders' Finish and Shingles, Presque Isle.—The number and variety of the articles coming under the head of builders' finish have greatly increased of late years, and a large and complete plant of the most improved machinery is now absolutely indispensable to the manufacture of a full line of such goods. The plant operated by Messrs. John Wilson & Son is strictly first-class and is very com-plete, so that that firm are prepared to furnish builders' finish of all kinds at very short notice and at the lowest prevailing rates. Shingles also are largely manufactured, and bottom prices will be quoted on all grades and on large and small lots. The firm is constituted of Messrs. John 'and Charles L. Wilson, and began business in Presque Isle in 1891, having formerly been located in Washburn. Their present mill is 50×60 feet in dimen-sions, is supplied with a 60-horse engine, and employ-ment is given to from six to ten assistants, so that the most extensive orders can be filled at comparatively short notice, as well as at prices as low as the lowest.

PHAIR HOTEL, James H. Phair, Proprietor, special attention given to Commercial Men, Presque Isle, Me.—If an experienced commercial traveler should be called upon to testify in court concerning the character of American hotels in general he might justly claim "expert" witness fees, for commercial men are certainly experts on that subject and therefore when they unite in endorsing a hotel it is perfectly safe to assume that that hotel is about "as good as they make 'em," the attending conditions being of course taken into consideration. The proprietor of the Phair Hotel gives special attention to commercial men and they return the compliment by giving special attention to the Phair Hotel which they pronounce one of the best-managed and most agreeable public houses in this section of the State. The owner and manager is Mr. James H. Phair, and commercial men in particular and the guests of the house in general are fond of declaring that the "phair" treatment they receive at his hands causes them to very pleasantly remember the hotel and to recommend it earnestly to all visitors to this vicinity. Mr. Phair was born in Maine, served in the army during the Rebellion, and inaugurated his present enterprise in 1884. The house can comfortably accommodate forty guests and is advantageously located, well furnished and well kept in every part. A free hack is run in connection with the house. The table is supplied with an abundance of good, substantial food, well cooked and neatly served ; and a sufficient number of assistants is employed to ensure prompt service to guests at all times.

A. R. GOULD, formerly of Bangor, is one of the prominent business men of the town ; indeed few men in the county are doing a more varied and extensive business, and probably none surpass him in enterprises that yield large returns of local benefit. Mr. Gould is of the type of men especially calculated to build up and improve his surroundings. As a business man he has a quick and clear judgment, ready and prompt decision, and very large executive ability. Added to these qualities he is by temperament highly liberal and enterprising. In short, Gould is broad-gauged and hustling, and as a natural result quite a successful man. He came from Bangor to Presque Isle some four years ago. His first important business move a year or so subsequently thereto, was his purchase from Hon. C. F. A. Johnson of the valuable saw mill property located on the Presque Isle stream, Bridge street. This mill is equipped with the most improved machinery for manufacturing all kinds of long and short lumber, and under Mr. Gould's management its capacity has been nearly or quite doubled. Its yearly output now runs up to several millions, most of which is shipped to Boston by rail. To his lumber business Mr. Gould last year added a brick yard, where he manufactures about one million brick annually. He employs several large crews during the winter season getting lumber to stock his mill with, and in its manufacture and in his other branches of business, he gives regular employment during the summer months to something like fifty men.

But it is in the line of real estate and land development that Mr. Gould's peculiar business instincts have been displayed most characteristically since settling in Presque Isle. Some two years since he purchased a tract of land lying on the west side of the Presque Isle stream, extending northward from Park street, and containing something over a hundred acres. This tract is quite centrally located, but previous to Mr. Gould's acquisition of it the only access to the portion of it available for desirable residence sites, was by a narrow and swampy way running northward from Bridge street, which served the double purpose of a lane for a cow pasture and a thoroughfare for the inhabitants of a number of ill kept shanties which bordered it. To this uninviting feature was added the fact that a small portion of the tract stretching northward from Park or Bridge street was low and wet, and the whole rough and disfigured by stumps, stones and bushes. But Mr. Gould's eye caught on to the possibilities of this tract. He saw in the long high ridge which stretched half a mile or more northward, following the windings of the smooth and pleasant stream, and falling in easy slopes and undulations to its bank, sightly and handsome lots for residences. He saw that the land could be cleared and smoothed and the wet part easily drained ; he saw also that a bridge could be thrown across the stream at a point that would make the best part of the tract readily and easily accessible from the principal street of the village. With such a man as Gould original and shrewd perception of an object to be attained is coupled with executive ability to bring it about, and the result is that within a year he had the stream spanned by a handsome bridge, the land thoroughly drained, largely cleared and smoothed, laid out into wide, straight streets, and divided into building-

lots. What was formerly a straggling lane has been transformed into a wide smooth street, running along for some distance on the west side of the stream, as straight as an arrow. Within the past year Mr. Gould has built a handsome and expensive residence for himself on a sightly point, around which a number of other neat houses are springing up, and all in all, "Gouldville," as it is termed, is the coming and growing section of the village. It is the place to which intending builders of homes in this thrifty village, and even those who are seeking investment in lots to sell again, will naturally turn both for the reason that the prospective growth of the village is here, and the consequent appreciation in value, and also from the fact that it is decidedly the best, pleasantest and most convenient residence section at present unoccupied. Furthermore, this locality is attractive to men of small means who desire to acquire homes on easy terms, from the fact that Mr. Gould proposes, in addition to putting the lots on the market at a reasonable price, to supply intending builders with brick and all kinds of lumber on easy terms of payment. This is a business policy by which both individuals and the public are largely benefited, and Mr. Gould deserves just credit, not only for the enterprise that has thrown open this large and eligible addition to the residence portion of the village, but also for the liberal business methods that make it available to those of moderate as well as large means.

S. H. WEYMAN, Wheelwright and Woodworker, Presque Isle, Me.—The schoolboy who said that "a wheelwright is a man who rights wheels," was not so far wrong as he might have been, and, indeed, was correct enough as far as he went, for an important part of a wheelwright's business most certainly is to "right," or put in order. wheels, but he must also be prepared to make wheels if necessary, and to make and repair the running gear of vehicles in general Mr. S. H. Weyman is prepared to do even more than this, for he is a general woodworker as well as a wheelwright, and has the facilities, the skill and the disposition to do first class work at short notice and at moderate rates. Mr. Weyman makes a specialty of the manufacture of jiggers. He is a native of New Brunswick and has carried on his present establishment since 1890. The premises made use of comprise two floors, each measuring 40×50 feet, and are fitted up with all necessary tools, etc , to enable operations to be carried on to excellent advantage. Repairing is given special attention, and will be done in a very neat and durable manner at low rates.

W. R. PIPES, Dry and Fancy Goods, Presque Isle, Me.—Every business establishment has a character of its own as surely as every individual has, and as the distinguishing characteristic of the enterprise carried on by Mr. W. R Pipes is reliability, it is natural that it should be very popular with the purchasing public, for all of us like to feel assured of getting what we pay for, and it is Mr. Pipe's invariable policy to represent his goods just as they are and return full value for money received He is a native of New Brunswick, and has been identified with his present enterprise for the past ten years. The premises occupied are located at No. 11 Main street, and are 22×60 feet in dimensions. The stock comprises dry and fancy goods, ladies' cloaks, boots and shoes, etc., and is the most complete in each department of any store of a similar nature in Presque Isle. All tastes and all purses can easily be suited. Mr. Pipes quotes prices as low as can be named on first-class goods, and with the help of three efficient assistants is enabled to give every caller immediate and courteous attention. Mr. Pipes began business in a small way, and by close attention to it together with his liberal methods of dealing with the public, he has succeeded in building up a prosperous and steadily growing patronage.

THE PRESQUE ISLE NATIONAL BANK,

Presque Isle, Me.—The Presque Isle National Bank commenced business January 2, 1888, so that the condition of affairs which led to its incorporation is still fresh in the minds of the public and needs no explanation here. Suffice it to say there was a general feeling that the great development of this section of late years and the strong probability of still greater development in the near future combined to make additional banking facilities absolutely necessary; and the results attained by the furnishing of such have, we believe, been perfectly satisfactory to all parties concerned and justified the predictions of those who most cordially favored the proposed institution Its facilities have been largely availed of, the individual deposits now aggregating about $100,000, and the fact that the surplus and undivided profits aggregated nearly $16,-000 as far back as November, 1890, is additional evidence of large business and hearty popular support as well as of prudent and able management, and the effect of this evidence is made even stronger by a study of the following report of the condition of the bank at the date mentioned, November 1, 1890.

Resources.

Loans and discounts........................	$115,767.84
U. S. bonds to secure circulation	12,500.00
Due from approved agents.................	25,357.62
Due from other national banks.............	1,608.58
Banking house furniture and fixtures.......	7,000.00
Current expenses and taxes paid.......... ...	479.83
Premium on U. S. bonds....................	2,500.00
Redemption fund with U. S. Treasurer......	562.50
Cash on hand.............................	14,278.48
	$180,054.85

Liabilities.

Capital stock paid in........................	$50,000.00
Surplus fund...............................	11,000.00
Undivided profits...........................	4,674.98
National bank notes outstanding.............	11,250.00
Dividends unpaid.........................	12.00
Individual deposits........................	99,953.00
Demand certificates of deposit..............	3,164.87
	$180,054.85

The institution is thoroughly well equipped for the carrying on of a general banking business, including the reception of deposits, collection of drafts, purchase and sale of standard securities, and the discounting of approved commercial paper; and it is prepared to receive the accounts of firms, of corporations, of institutions and of individuals on the most favorable terms, and to give prompt and careful attention to all business placed in its hands. The officers and directors are men thoroughly identified with the advancement of the best interests of this section, as will be seen by the following list: J. W. Bolton, president; G. H. Freeman, vice-president; A. II. Jenks, cashier Directors: James W. Bolton, George H. Freeman, Morril N. Drew, Jarvis Hayward, Luman S. Judd, Llewellyn Powers, Chas. F. Daggett, Thos. H. Phair, William C. Spaulding.

L. I. WHEELER, manufacturer of Sleighs and Wagons, Horse Shoeing a Specialty, Presque Isle, Me.— The chances are that a great many owners and users of sleighs and wagons are included among our readers, and the establishment carried on by Mr. L. I. Wheeler, in this town, is of special interest to this class, for Mr. Wheeler is a carriage manufacturer and blacksmith, and has improved facilities at hand for the doing of such work, making a specialty of horseshoeing. He is a native of Pittsfield, Me., and has been identified with his present enterprise since 1890, though the shop, has been established for many years previously. The premises made use of include a carriage and blacksmith shop of the dimensions 40×50 feet, both being completely fitted up, and employment being given to three experienced assistants, so that orders can be filled at short notice—a point that will be especially appreciated by those who want a wagon or sleigh repaired and cannot afford to be long deprived of the use of it. The work done here is dependable in the full sense of the word, for selected material is used, and the workmanship is first-class throughout, while his prices are reasonable for such kind of work.

G. A. COOK, Wholesale and Retail dealer in Groceries and Provisions, Bolton Block, Bridge Street, Presque Isle, Me.—There is a familiar old saying to the effect that a stream cannot rise higher than its source, and it is equally true that the retail establishment devoted to any special line of business cannot offer first-class inducements if they are obliged to depend upon second-class wholesale houses to furnish them with their supplies. It is therefore clear that every resident of Presque Isle and vicinity is directly interested in the character of the local wholesale grocery houses, for groceries rank with the necessities of life and it is of the first importance to be able to buy them to the best possible advantage. The business carried on by Mr. G. A. Cook, may justly be regarded as the representative wholesale and retail grocery house of this town, for the enterprise conducted by him, is of long and honorable standing, having been carried on since 1882. Extensive premises are occupied at corner of Bridge and Main streets, in the Bolton Block, and consists of a store 36×80 feet in dimensions, together with an oil and flour cellar, and a very large stock is carried at all times, being made up of staple groceries and provisions, oil, etc., etc., and being remarkably complete in every department. Mr. Cook, who is a native of Ellsworth, Me., is in a position to easily meet all honorable competition, for he enjoys most favorable relations with producers and has a well-earned reputation for quoting bottom prices, as well as for handling goods that will please the most select trade.

RAMAIN MICHAUD, dealer in Meats, Fish and Vegetables of all kinds, No. 4 Bridge Street, Presque Isle, Me.—There is probably no housekeeper but what has experienced more or less difficulty in obtaining entirely satisfactory meats, for the payment of the highest market rates by no means assures the purchaser of getting first-class goods, as many of our readers undoubtedly know from practical experience. This is not always the fault of the dealer, for mistakes are sure to happen in every line of business, and sometimes these mistakes are entirely excusable, but nevertheless it is perfectly safe to say that, generally speaking, those who are willing to pay for high grade meats should be able to depend upon being supplied with such, and in this connection we may very fittingly call attention to the facilities offered by Mr. Ramain Michaud at No. 4 Bridge street, for here may always be found a first class assortment of fresh meats, and those who want choice cuts of beef, mutton or lamb, should by all means give this popular establishment a call. Mr. Michaud gives personal attention to the filling of orders, besides employing a number of efficient assistants, so that callers are sure of prompt and polite service. Fresh fish and vegetables of all kinds are largely dealt in, and the prices quoted will be found strictly in accordance with the lowest market rates. In connection with this business Mr. Michaud has a slaughter house located near the trotting park, where he keeps from twenty to fifty hogs the year round, and slaughters about one and one half tons per week of meats of all kinds, besides butchering a large amount for the public.

H. C. REDMAN, Livery and Feed Stable, Presque Isle, Me.—The majority of those who patronize livery stables are not unreasonable and therefore do not expect to be furnished with horses that can trot in 2:50, or with carriages that look as though they never had been used, but even the best-natured customer may be excused for kicking when he is supplied with the lame apology for a horse, and the antediluvian vehicle which some public stable keepers seem to think ought to be entirely satisfactory. It is very poor policy to force patrons to put up with such "accommodations," for it has a tendency to disgust them with hiring teams, and to cause them either to give up driving or to get a turnout of their own. We think that the methods followed by Mr. H. C. Redman might be profitably imitated by some other stable keepers whom we could name, for he spares no pains to keep a sufficiency of desirable teams on hand for livery purposes, and, although he makes no extravagant claims, still, his rigs will compare favorably with the average private turnouts in this vicinity. Mr. Redman is a native of this State, and succeeded to his present business in 1888. The premises utilized are spacious, and measure 36×110 feet, being well arranged, and include accommodations for some forty horses. A general livery and feed business is done, and employment is given to efficient assistants so that all orders are assured immediate and careful attention, and the charges are moderate.

ACADEMY STREET CARRIAGE FACtory, Carriages and Sleighs manufactured and repaired, J. G. Hilt & Son, Presque Isle, Me.—Since Mr. J. G. Hilt began the manufacturing and repairing of carriages and sleighs, etc., on Academy street, some years ago, his work has become so thoroughly and favorably known to the residents of Presque Isle, that nothing we can say concerning it will be new to them, but as this book will circulate widely in other sections, we take pleasure in making prominent mention of Mr. Hilt's productions in the hope of inducing those who need a strictly reliable vehicle to investigate the advantages he offers. He has had long and varied experience in the carriage business, and allows no imperfect work to leave his shop with his knowledge. Only first class workmen are employed and none but the best of materials used, good, honest work and a thorough job every time for a moderate price. Mr. Hilt is also the owner for the county of the automatic wagon brake, and for the town of Presque Isle for the sled brake, and is prepared to fit them onto wagons and sleds. A single trial will convince anyone of the superiority of these brakes. On April 1, 1891, Mr. Frank E. Hilt, the son, was admitted to partnership. The firm have recently added steam power and machinery to facilitate the production of their work.

COX & GRAVES, Grocers and dealers in Cracked Corn, Corn Meal, Flour, Buckwheat Flour, Mixed Feed of all Kinds, Wholesale and Retail, Presque Isle, Me.—It is unnecessary to dwell upon the importance of being able to purchase grain, flour and feed, etc., in any desired quantities at the lowest market rates, for the advantages derived from an enterprise which has for its object the furnishing of an abundant and dependable supply of those staple commodities at bottom prices, are so obvious as to be understood by every member of the community. Therefore it goes without saying that the establishment conducted by Messrs. Cox and Graves, is popular throughout this vicinity, for they do a large retail business and wholesale as well in cracked corn, corn meal, flour, buckwheat flour, and mixed feed of all kinds, all supplied from the finely equipped grist mill, run by water power, conducted by the senior member of this firm, Mr. S. Cox. So that the proprietors are in a position to meet all honorable competition in their line of business, filling the most extensive orders at short notice and always quoting prices in accordance with the lowest market rates. A well stocked grocery store is also carried on by this enterprising firm, and is 25×40 feet in dimensions, while the grist mill is conveniently located, and employment given to four efficient assistants. Mr. Cox, is a native of New Brunswick, and Mr. Graves of this town, and started this enterprise in 1888, since which time an extensive patronage has been built up.

A. E. WIGHT, Real Estate Agent, Main Street, Presque Isle, Me.—The real estate business conducted by Mr. A. E. Wight on Main street, was founded in 1890, so that the public have had ample opportunity to become conversant with Mr. Wight's methods, and to judge intelligently concerning his facilities and ability. That the verdict is distinctly favorable is evidenced by the present magnitude of his business, and indeed but few inquiries are necessary in order to demonstrate the fact that Mr. Wight is considered a competent authority on real estate matters, making his coöperation of great value to those seeking dependable and "inside" information concerning this class of property. His office is on Main street, and as he always has on his books some very desirable real estate, to sell, rent, or exchange, those wishing to invest in, to dispose of, or to hire a house, store, or tenement, may save themselves time, trouble, and perhaps money, by taking advantage of the facilities here provided. Information will be cheerfully and courteously given, and we are confident our readers will have reason to thank us for calling their attention to this popular agency.

HISTORICAL SKETCH OF FORT FAIRFIELD.

A township map of Aroostook county has an even, regular and conventional appearance in striking contrast with that of maps of most other New England counties, and also in marked contrast with the actual appearance of the wild and beautiful country comprised within its limits, for Aroostook county is divided into many square townships of equal size so that a map of it resembles a checker board instead of looking like "crazy patchwork," as the colored maps of nearly all other counties in the New England states do. So universal are these equal squares throughout the county that any exception to them at once attracts the attention of even a casual observer, and so it is that Fort Fairfield is one of the first townships to catch the eye, for it is oblong instead of square in shape, it being made up of two townships, one directly north of the other. The natural inference would be that this is an especially important town and this inference would be found on further investigation to be strictly correct, for Fort Fairfield is one of the most prosperous towns in Aroostook county—which is equivalent to saying that it is one of the most prosperous in New England as Aroostook county is enjoying at least as high a degree of prosperity as any other section of " Yankeeland."

Fort Fairfield is a border town and owes its warlike name to that circumstance, for during the "Aroostook war," caused by dispute concerning the boundary line between the United States and British America, a military post was established within the limits of the present township and a fort was erected for the purpose of better enabling the troops to repel the expected invasion. But, as our readers are doubtless aware, the "Aroostook war" was an almost entirely bloodless struggle in spite of its formidable name, and the early annals of Fort Fairfield are happily free from the stain of any blood other than that of the bears, wolves, catamounts and other "varmints" that disputed the efforts of the pioneer settlers to establish a home in the wilderness. The fort was named in honor of John Fairfield who was governor at the time of its erection. The history of the township covers a period of just about three-quarters of a century, the first settlements having been made about 1816 by people from the adjacent province of New Brunswick, but for all practical purposes the birth of the town occurred in 1858, for it was incorporated March 11th of that year, having at that time just about doubled the population of 401 which it had at the beginning of the decade, or in 1850. In 1860 the population had increased to 901 and an even larger proportionate gain was made from 1860 to 1870 in spite of the deterring influences of the civil war, Fort Fairfield's population in 1870 amounting to 1,893. The succeeding decade witnessed another pronounced gain, the population in 1880 having been 2,807, and the 1890 census gives the town a population of 3,526, so it will be seen that its progress is constantly "upward and onward." The increase in valuation during the past thirty years has been even more remarkable. In 1860 the valuation of estates in town was $75,975.00. During the next ten years a phenomenal gain was made, the estates in 1870 being valued at $276,800.00. In 1880 the estate valuation had risen to $468,471.00, and in 1890 to $893,593.00.

We give herewith an illustration of the residence of E. E. Scates, which is one of the finest in Fort Fairfield. It is situated on Fort Hill and commands a fine view of the river and the surrounding country. It is heated with hot air and hot water, and has hot water throughout the house. Mr. S. D. Beckwith was the architect, which is a sufficient guarantee that the house is well arranged. We present a fine cut of this handsome residence.

The town's surface is uneven and there is an abundance of beautiful scenery in town, but there are no high hills and the soil is easily tilled and is wonderfully productive, this town holding the record for the largest crop of potatoes per acre ever raised in the

RESIDENCE OF E. E. SCATES.

east. The record rests on no man's "say so" but was established by official count which placed the yield from one acre at 745 bushels and 25 pounds. The potatoes were raised by Mr. Philo Reed, who lives about two miles from Fort Fairfield village. This banner crop was produced in 1890 and was sold to Messrs. Thurlough & Richards of Fort Fairfield at the rate of $2.15 per barrel. Potato raising and potato shipping are so largely engaged in by residents of Fort Fairfield and have so important a bearing upon its influence and development that no apology is necessary for introducing the following article, condensed from the town's lively and well edited local newspaper, *The Fort Fairfield Gazette*:

"Aroostook and potatoes have become almost synonymous terms, to such a high place in the estimation of consumers and wholesale dealers in seed, have potatoes grown in our fertile valley of Aroostook attained ; and if the county ever adorns its official documents with a county seal, the hand hoe and potato digger ought certainly to occupy a conspicuous place. Going back some 20 years, the chief, and in fact only source by which ready money was attainable, was made by hauling produce to Bangor markets and supplying the lumber camps. Those were days many of our farmers remembered as the 'good old times.' They paid $15.00 for a barrel of flour and 25 cents per pound for pork, and received $6.00 per bushel for herds grass, then their most paying crop. 1876 was the year in which the first potato crop of any size was planted, and in 1882 the high price of $3.25 per barrel was paid. This gave an impetus to the trade which it has never lost, but in the following year, '83, they were only worth 35 cents per barrel, and upwards of ten car loads were shipped to Houlton to make starch at 30 cents per barrel ; an event which is not likely to happen again, with three starch factories in town. But with these discouragements, early frosts and individual failures taken into account, the Aroostook farmer justly believes in potatoes, and the season which is just closing, and that which has just begun, for they overlap each other, will make the greatest advance which has yet been made.

"Through the courtesy of the potato buyers, we are enabled to give the following figures which we believe to be thoroughly correct and reliable :

"Total amount paid, $445,308.00 ; total amount of barrels shipped, 203,370 ; average amount paid per barrel, $2.25 ; highest price paid, $3.75 ; length of season, forty-one weeks.

"Amount paid for potatoes for starch included in above, $30,000.00.

"This gives the remarkable average of $1,810.19 per working day, paid in cash to our farmers.

"The following figures are interesting and help to give some idea of what our farmers receive in cash for potatoes alone :

MAIN STREET, FORT FAIRFIELD.

"The area of the township is 46,080 acres. About one-third of this is under cultivation ; this gives us 15,360 acres, and taking ten per cent as the amount of land occupied by potatoes last year ; this gives us 1536 acres in potatoes, which divided into $445,308 gives us $289.91 per acre, but this, evidently, is too much. It is in fact about double the average amount per acre.

"This brings us to the conclusion that Fort Fairfield is the centre of trade for an area, which is, at the least, twice the size of its own township. Again we have about 904 polls, multiply this by two as we did with the acreage ; this gives 1,210, which divided into $445,308.00 gives $368.00 per year, or more than $1.00 per day to every poll in an area at least 12 miles by 12 or double the size of our own township.

"We think from the above we are justified in saying 'Aroostook' and 'potato' are synonymous."

Additional evidence of Fort Fairfield's great importance as a centre of production and distribution is afforded by the fact that more than 1,300 loaded cars were sent from this station during the past year—an average of more than four per day for every working day in the year. Manufacturing is largely carried on and there are some excellent water powers in town, these being on streams tributary to the Aroostook River which enters the town near its northwest corner, flows southeast to Fort Fairfield village and then turns to the northeast and leaves the township at a point nearly opposite that at which it entered. A few miles from the New Brunswick line the Aroostook loses its identity as a river, its point of junction with the river St. John being but a short distance from the Fort Fairfield boundary. The principal streams which flow into the Aroostook during its passage through the township are Johnston, Lovely, Grey and Hurd Brooks and Fitzherbert's Stream ; the chief water powers being furnished by the last named water course and by Lovely Brook, and among the establishments whose machinery is driven by them may be mentioned a long lumber mill, a grist mill, a wool carding mill, a woodworking mill, and a starch factory. Other streams passing through Fort Fairfield are Livingstone River which crosses its north-east corner and receives a good-sized tributary from the west ; and the River De Chute which also receives a tributary stream from the township and which crosses its south-west corner.

AROOSTOOK FALLS.
(Jam of Seven Million Feet of Logs.)

The manufacturing establishments of the town are by no means confined to those run by water-power, there being several large steam mills, one of which produces about 15,000,000 shingles annually, and another turns out half a million per week. There are also smaller mills, factories and shops of various kinds, and the articles produced at Fort Fairfield include lumber (long and short), bark, barrels, heading, staves, starch, shoddy, carriages, coffins and caskets, meal and feed, harnesses, steam boilers, plaster, iron and steel goods including cranks, axles, pitch-forks, blocks, etc., wagon brakes, general wood work, etc. A considerable portion of the township is heavily wooded, there being a very large amount of the best quality of birch and maple growth suitable for flooring, orange boxes, veneering, and other hard wood articles. The utilization of this growth is only a question of time and of no very long time either, and it is probable that Fort Fairfield will eventually become as famous as a manufacturing as she now is as an agricultural centre.

The local trade interests of the town in general, and of the village in particular, are also destined to become very extensive, they being already of very considerable importance and the village containing some of the largest and most elaborately fitted up stores in eastern Maine. Fort Fairfield's merchants are enterprising and aggressive but not speculative in their methods, and the wisdom of their management and the value of the opportunities open to them are indicated by the fact that there has not been a business failure in town for upwards of thirteen years — a record hard to match among communities equal to that of Fort Fairfield in size and in the number of commercial enterprises.

More than thirty substantial buildings were erected in the village and vicinity during the past season and this record is not exceptional but may be accepted as a fair example of the present rate of growth of this energetic town.

Fort Fairfield has enjoyed railway facilities since 1875, it being on the branch of the New Brunswick Railroad which has its terminus at Presque Isle. The town possesses many of the characteristics of a modern American city, such as extensive and well equipped mercantile establishments, large mills and factories, numerous school edifices among which is a handsome and commodious high school building, fine churches, and elegant residences. It is supplied with water and is illuminated by the Frontier Water and Electric Light Company, the service being excellent in every respect, and property is protected by a well equipped fire department of which G. E. Jewett is chief engineer.

The town offers many advantageous openings to capitalists, manufacturers, farmers and merchants; it is growing rapidly, steadily and substantially, and by the time the coming century opens. will probably have attained such large development and changed so materially in every way as to have fully justified even the most sanguine predictions of those who fully appreciate the many advantages. it now controls.

Representative Business Men of Fort Fairfield, Me.

SCATES & CO., dealers in Drugs, Medicines and Chemicals, Brushes, Sponges, Soaps, Toilet Articles, Books, Stationery, Fort Fairfield, Me.—One of the establishments in which the residents of Fort Fairfield put great confidence, is that which is conducted under the name of Scates & Co , for during the years that this enterprise has been carried on it has been managed in a straightforward manner that is worthy of unreserved commendation. This establishment was originally started by Mr. J. Dufton in 1879, and came into the possession of the present proprietor, Mr. E. E. Scates, in 1880 He is a native of Gorham, N. H. He has been clerk of the village corporation, is secretary Fort Fairfield Sewerage Co., and member of Board of Health. He occupies the corner store in Cutts' new block and has one of the finest drug stores in the State, it being finished in butternut, has marble tile floor, French plate windows, etc. It has two entrances, one on Main street and one on Fort Mill street. An immense quantity of drugs, medicines, chemicals, etc., are sold in the course of a year, and the purity and freshness of the articles used in compounding prescriptions, causes this establishment to be very generally patronized by those having such orders to fill. There is no element of chance allowed to enter into the operation of the prescription department at this store, for the most improved facilities are provided, and only skilled and experienced assistants are employed. The charges made are always reasonable, being as low as is consistent with the invariable use of the best materials. Prompt and efficient assistants are in attendance, and annoying delays are therefore of very rare occurrence. The stock constantly dealt in includes in addition to drugs, medicines, chemicals, etc., brushes, sponges, soaps, toilet articles, and books, stationery, also fine cigars and tobacco. The following are the specialties prepared at this pharmacy : Dr. Gold's Royal Balsam, cures coughs, colds, croup, and all throat and lung troubles ; stops that troublesome cough at night. Dr. Gold's Preservative Tooth Powder, prevents the teeth from decaying, removes tartar and makes them white. Dr. Hooper's Scratch Ointment, best in the world for scratches and old sores ; try it and you will use no other for your horses. Dr. Hooper's Cathartic Pills, cure all liver troubles; they are a safe, pleasant and agreeable family physic. Dr. Hooper's Worm Powders, a sure, safe and reliable worm expeller; the most easily administered to children of all ages of any worm medicine on the market. Dr. Hooper's Condition Powders : every farmer should have a package in his stable. Scate's Magic Corn and Wart Remover is a safe, speedy and painless cure for corns, bunions and callouses.

GOODHUE THE JEWELER, Holiday Novelties, Watches, Clocks, Jewelry, Silverware, Room Paper, Curtains, Sporting and Fancy Goods, Fort Fairfield, Me.—The name of "Goodhue the Jeweler," might be fittingly changed to "Good value the Jeweler," it a name characteristic of the business policy of its owner were needed, for there is no jeweler in the State who gives better value in all lines of goods, but the residents of this section will bear that fact in mind without being reminded of it by any change in name, and it would certainly be poor policy to alter a name so widely and favorably known as the one in question. The business carried on under it was founded in 1859 by Mr. I. W. Goodhue, who settled at Fort Fairfield after being a number of years in the jewelry business in Bangor. He began in a small way and it was not until after the building of the railroad in 1874 that conditions were such as to give opportunity for pronounced growth. In 1879 Mr. Goodhue removed from the lower to what is now the main village, but in less than a year was burned out and then took a small store in the Dresser Block. In 1883 Mr. A. F. Goodhue took an interest in the business, which was at once removed to the Collins House block, and within two years the growth of trade made it necessary to occupy the adjoining store also. The present premises have four large show windows and two entrances, and are almost as attractive without as within but not quite, for Mr. Goodhue carries the largest stock in Aroostook, and it is skillfully chosen and tastefully displayed, and so varied that all tastes and purses can be suited. We cannot describe it, but will simply say that Mr. Goodhue's specialties are watches, clocks, jewelry, silver ware, stationery, room paper, curtains, sporting and fancy goods, and an exceptionally full line of holiday novelties at the proper season. Very low prices are quoted on all the articles dealt in, but most important of all is the fact—well known of course to many of our readers—that every article, large or small, costly or cheap, bought here will prove just as represented in every respect. The above firm do more repairing on watches, clocks, jewelry, musical instruments, etc., etc., than any other place in Aroostook, and the proof of this statement is that three first-class workmen are at the bench the most of the time, some of whom have the experience of over forty years. All work intrusted to their care receive their best attention and is fully guaranteed to give perfect satisfaction in every respect or money refunded. They also have the only regular jewelry safe in the county, weighing 5430 pounds, where all articles left for repairs are deposited each night, guaranteeing perfect safety to their customers.

THURLOUGH & RICHARDS, Wholesale and Retail Grocers and General Commission Merchants, Fort Fairfield, Me.—Comparatively few of us are able to judge of the merits of groceries before using them, and even those who are competent to do so do not care to minutely examine every article submitted to them before accepting it, and therefore it is obvious that, other things being equal, the dealer who is entirely trustworthy and who takes pains to see that his customers get just what they pay for, will build up the largest as well as the most desirable patronage. This being the case there is no occasion for surprise at the extensive business done by Messrs. Thurlough & Richards, for these gentlemen have been identified with their present business since 1889, and are successors to the firm of E. Merritt & Son, this store having been a branch of their Houlton establishment. The individual members of the firm are Mr. F. A. Thurlough, Mr. J. M. Thurlough and Mr. H. G. Richards, all of whom are natives of Maine, and well known throughout Fort Fairfield and vicinity. In view of their experience it is superfluous to say they are thoroughly familiar with their business in every detail. They are naturally proud of the honorable record of their establishment and it will be no fault of theirs if the service rendered in the future is not even more economical and efficient than that extended in the past. The premises made use of are 30×150 feet in dimensions and contain a heavy and varied stock, for Messrs. Thurlough & Richards are wholesale and retail grocers and general commission merchants, they being very extensively engaged in the shipping of potatoes. During the potato season of 1890 this firm paid out $83,000 for potatoes (including the pay for labor of handling them) and which took 223 cars to transport, they being shipped to various Western points. Four capable assistants being employed, and particular attention is paid to the requirements of family trade, all orders being promptly filled, and every article guaranteed to prove as represented.

FRENCH BROS., dealers in Dry and Fancy Goods, Fort Fairfield, Me.—It is a heavy and a varied stock that is offered by French Bros., but after all, the highest praise that can be accorded it, is that all the many articles comprising it can be confidently guaranteed to prove as represented. The establishment in question was founded about 1876, by E. M. Dresser, who was succeeded by the present firm in 1886. Messrs. French Brothers have won a high place in the confidence of the purchasing public, for they make it an invariable rule to sell goods strictly on their merits, and display great enterprise in catering to all classes of trade. Messrs. A. O. and G. L. French are both natives of Sangerville, Me., and are extremely well known personally throughout Fort Fairfield and vicinity. The premises occupied comprise a store about 1500 square feet in dimensions, containing a stock of dry and fancy goods, millinery, cloaks, etc., embracing the latest novelties in its various departments, the prices named on the same being as low as the lowest. Employment is given to four competent and courteous assistants and goods will be cheerfully shown at any time. This is a truly representative establishment, and its high standing is creditable alike to the proprietor and to the community that give practical proof of their appreciation of honorable and enterprising methods.

F. C. BOLSTER, Manufacturer of Wagons and Sleds: Blacksmithing: Fort Fairfield, Me.—It is the simplest thing in the world to buy a cheap carriage but it is by no means so simple and easy to buy a carriage cheap, and hence we feel that we are doing our readers a service when we advise them to call upon Mr. F. C. Bolster when they wish anything in the wagon or sled line for this gentleman not only quotes low prices but he furnishes vehicles that will prove just as represented in every

respect. Mr. Bolster is a native of Sangerville, Me., and served in the army during the Rebellion. He established his present business at Fort Fairfield in 1857, he being the only mechanic in business now that was in business here at that time, and is thoroughly familiar with the manufacture of wagons and sleds as well as blacksmithing in all its details. He utilizes premises covering an area of 625 square feet, which is fitted up with every requisite facility for the manufacture, painting and repairing of all kinds of vehicles, as well as every description of blacksmithing. Employment is given to a sufficient force of assistants, and every department of the business is carefully supervised; no pains being spared to satisfy every patron and to deliver orders promptly at the time promised in all cases.

WM. SMALL & CO., General Store; Furniture and Carpets a specialty; Fort Fairfield, Me.—A very considerable proportion of those buying house furnishing goods are comparatively unfamiliar with the value of such articles, and hence must depend upon the integrity of the concern with which they do business for assurance that they will be given full value for all they are required to expend. For this reason it is but common sense to use careful discrimination before deciding where to place such orders, and we take pleasure in aiding our readers to arrive at a perfectly satisfactory decision by calling to their attention the facilities possessed by Messrs. Wm. Small & Co., for this firm not only have an enviable reputation for fair dealing, but they carry a stock and quote prices which enable them to easily meet all honorable competition. The partners are Messrs. Wm. Small, a native of Maine, and C. W. Johnston, of New Brunswick. Both these gentlemen are widely and favorably known throughout Fort Fairfield, Mr. Small having been selectman, while Mr. Johnston served in the army during the Rebellion, and has been town clerk. This firm keep a general store, making a specialty of furniture, carpets, etc. Upholstering is also done in the best manner and at low rates. The premises utilized comprise three floors and a basement, each 30×100 feet in dimensions, and no one wishing house furnishings of any kind should neglect giving it a call, as time, money and trouble may be saved by doing so. Employment is given to thoroughly competent assistants, and orders will be filled in an accurate and painstaking manner at short notice, and at the lowest market rates.

HOPKINS BROTHERS, dealers in Meats, Groceries and Provisions, Fort Fairfield, Me.—In order to carry on a really first-class market it is necessary to offer a carefully selected, as well as a large and varied stock, and the excellent reputation attained by the establishment conducted by Messrs. Hopkins Brothers is largely due to the care exercised in choosing only such articles as are adapted to first-class family trade. Messrs. Jas. R. and Eben S. Hopkins are both natives of Fort Fairfield, and have been identified with the meat and provision business since 1881, and located at their present establishment since 1886. They now command a very desirable trade, for not only are their goods equal to the best in every respect but their prices are as low as can be quoted on articles of standard quality. The premises made use of cover an area of 3,000 square feet, and contain a fine assortment of all kinds of meats, groceries, and provisions. Messrs. Hopkins Brothers are also dealers in live and dressed stock, fresh and salt fish, fruit, vegetables, etc., and have their own slaughter house and farm. It has been their aim from the first to completely satisfy every customer, and they have certainly spared no pains to do so, both as regards the quality of the articles offered and the prices quoted on them. An extensive business is transacted and eight well informed assistants are employed, and every customer is assured prompt as well as courteous attention.

G. E. BARTLETT & CO., dealers in Dry Goods, Boots and Shoes, etc ; lowest prices in Aroostook ; Fort Fairfield, Me.—The establishment now conducted under the firm name of G. E. Bartlett & Co was founded in 1886, and has become very widely and favorably known throughout Fort Fairfield, for the policy of the concern from the very first has been to give full value for money received, selling goods strictly on their merits and fully guaranteeing them to prove as represented. Such a policy when consistently and persistently carried out can have but one effect, and the enviable reputation of this firm proves that they have put the principle in question into practical operation. They carry a large and complete stock of dry and fancy goods, also a fine line of boots and shoes, the prices being guaranteed right in each department of the business. This fine new store is conveniently located, and is 24×70 feet in dimensions. It has a fine plate glass window where one can see an attractive display of dress goods, etc., which is often renewed with fresh novelties. The proprietor, Mr. G. E. Bartlett, is a native of Bangor, Me., and very well known throughout Fort Fairfield and vicinity. He makes it a rule to give all orders received immediate and careful attention, carrying a stock complete in every department, containing goods suitable for both sexes and all ages, and particular attention is paid to handling footwear that is not clumsy and stiff, but yet is strong and enduring. The dry goods department also contains many novelties and fashionable goods to choose from. Those who prefer plain goods will find articles suited to their taste. Three assistants are employed, and callers are assured prompt and polite attention.

J. H. WALLACE, Artist Photographer ; all kinds of Photographic Work done in the most artistic manner by the new Instantaneous Process ; no trouble to get the most perfect pictures of children by this process ; Pictures Enlarged and Framed ; Viewing a specialty ; Perkins Block, Fort Fairfield, Me.—During the trial of a case in the supreme court a few months ago one "expert" witness testified that there was "an almost endless number of photographers in this country, but only comparatively few photographic artists." Of course, from the very nature of things it is often difficult to distinguish true art from false, and pretence from solid merit, but, nevertheless, any intelligent person can appreciate a good portrait, especially when they are thoroughly familiar with the features of the original, and therefore it is not surprising that the photographic studio of Mr. J. H. Wallace should be one of the most popular in this section, for the uniform excellence of the work turned out during the many years that Mr. Wallace has practiced his profession in Fort Fairfield, has naturally attracted the favorable attention of not only residents but out-of-town people as well. Although of long standing the establishment is fitted up with improved apparatus. All kinds of photographic work is done in the most artistic manner by the instantaneous process, it being no trouble to get the most perfect pictures of children by this method. A specialty is made of all kinds of copying and enlarging, and a fine line of specimen work including crayon, India ink, water color, oil ferrotype, etc., etc., may be seen by calling at his studio. A stock of the latest styles of mouldings is kept constantly on hand from which frames are manufactured to order. You will also find there a good line of Fort Fairfield views, and viewing of all kinds will be done for you on short notice. Mr. Wallace commenced business in this town about six years ago in Perkins Block, where he has done business until about a year ago. The place he now occupied on Main street was built especially for his business, and some admirable specimens of photograpic work may be found therein. Mr. Wallace is a native of Millbridge, Me., and has gained a high reputation as an artist photographer throughout Fort Fairfield and vicinity. The Fort Fairfield views illustrated in this book were taken by Mr. Wallace.

H. KNIGHT, Dealer in Groceries and Provisions ; also Shipper of Aroostook Potatoes and Eastern Eggs, Fort Fairfield, Me.—Prominent among the most enterprising business houses in Fort Fairfield is that conducted by Mr. H. Knight, who is engaged in the carrying on of an establishment devoted to the sale of staple and fancy groceries, provisions, etc. This house was originally founded in 1880, by its present proprietor, Mr. Knight is a native of Vermont, and is extremely well known and highly esteemed throughout this town, as a dealer in groceries, etc. He has built up a large retail trade, which is annually increasing, and to those who have inspected his goods and prices this seems but the natural and inevitable result of the excellence of the one and the lowness of the other. The store is centrally located and is of the dimensions of 30×125 feet. A very extensive and desirable assortment is shown, comprising staple and fancy groceries, fresh provisions, etc. Mr. Knight deals in lamps, crockery ware, etc., and is also a shipper of Aroostook potatoes and Eastern eggs, all of which are offered at the lowest market rates. Thoroughly reliable assistants are employed, thus insuring prompt and accurate service to all customers, while goods are delivered free to any part of the town.

THE FORT FAIRFIELD DRUG STORE, Palmer & Holmes, Fort Fairfield, Me.—"The Fort Fairfield Drug Store," conducted by Messrs. Palmer & Holmes, is so generally and favorably known throughout this vicinity that commendation of it will appear quite superfluous to many of our readers, but a review of the representative business enterprises of this town to be complete must necessarily include mention of this well managed and popular establishment. The business was founded in 1890 by the present firm, who are not only thoroughly familiar with every detail of the enterprise, but meets with notable success in fully maintaining the high standard associated with it. Owing to the increase of their business this firm have recently removed to the large and commodious store formerly occupied by G. E. Bartlett & Co., situated next to H. N. Goodhue's grocery. The store is 24×65 feet in size and is thoroughly fitted up, especially in the prescription department, for particular attention is given to the prompt and accurate compounding of prescriptions, and the assortment of drugs, medicines and chemicals, is so complete that all orders can be filled without delay, every precaution being taken to ensure absolute accuracy in every detail of the work. A full line of druggists' sundries, also books and stationery, together with a fine line of silverware and jewelry are carried in stock, and the prices are always in strict accordance with the lowest market rates. Messrs. T. H. Palmer, and H. C. Holmes are both natives of New Brunswick, and are well known in Fort Fairfield as energetic and representative business men.

McGILL BROTHERS, Grist Mill and Carding Mill, Fort Fairfield, Me.—A grist mill is always a great convenience and so is a carding mill, hence the establishment carried on by Messrs. McGill Brothers is a decided public benefit, as it combines a grist mill, a planing mill and a carding mill, and is very liberally and intelligently managed ; the machinery being kept in first-class condition and the best of work being done at reasonable rates. The present firm succeeded Mr. J. Averill in 1889, and is composed of Messrs. W. E., John E. and James A. McGill, all of whom are natives of New Brunswick. The premises made use of are 30×60 feet in size, and three stories in height, and the machinery is run by both steam and water power, so orders can be promptly filled at all times. Besides doing custom grinding and wool carding the firm deal in grain and mill feed, quoting uniformly low rates and carrying a sufficiently large stock to enable them to fill orders without delay. A specialty is made of planing, jig sawing and splitting.

W. A. HAINES, manufacturer and dealer in Lumber, Flour, Feed and Plaster, Shipping Bark, Fort Fairfield, Me.—Mr. W. A. Haines is a one of the most active and best known business men in this section of the State. The undertaking carried on by him was formerly conducted by Messrs. H. A. Haines & Son, the present proprietor assuming sole control in 1888. He is a manufacturer and dealer in lumber, flour, feed and plaster, and also deals largely in bark, shipping it in large quantities, and being in a position to furnish it at the lowest market rates. For many years a lumber business alone was carried on, but some eight years ago a grist mill was added, and this department of the business has since reached large proportions. Mr. Haines sells lumber, flour, feed and plaster at both wholesale and retail, and has the reputation of furnishing dependable goods at bottom rates, a reputation which he well deserves and steadily maintains, by giving close personal attention to all the many details of his business. Employment is given to from seven to ten assistants, and all orders large and small are promptly and carefully filled.

S. F. LORD, manufacturer of Harnesses and dealer in Whips, Blankets, etc., Fort Fairfield, Me.—The establishment now conducted by Mr. S. F. Lord is one of the best known of its kind in town. It was originally founded many years ago by Mr. A. W. Rogers, who was succeeded in 1881 by the firm of Rogers & Lord, the present proprietor assuming full control in 1882. Mr. S. F. Lord is a native of Belgrade, Me., and has gained the reputation for being a skillful harness maker, and for being able to compete, in the excellence of his work, with houses of much longer standing. The line of trade comprises the manufacture of fine harness of all kinds. He also keeps an assortment of whips, blankets, etc., and everything that goes to make up a comprehensive and complete stock of horse furnishings. The business is entirely retail. The store covers an area of 600 square feet. A specialty is made of custom and repair work, which is neatly and promptly done. Mr. Lord uses none but good stock. He employs well-trained assistants, and neglects no means to assure satisfaction to his customers, both as regards the quality of the work done, and the promptness with which orders are filled. The charges are uniformly moderate, and we feel sure that all dealings with this gentleman will be entirely satisfactory.

JEWELL B. WILLIAMS, dealer in Clothing, Boots, Shoes, Hats, Caps, etc.; also Livery; Fort Fairfield, Me.—Some of us care more for comfort than for style when choosing foot-wear, clothing, hats, caps, etc. Others desire the very latest novelties, no matter what they may be, others put durability before everything else, and still others strive to obtain those that are at once stylish, comfortable and durable, so it will be seen that a dealer who really caters successfully to all classes of trade, must of necessity carry a very large and varied stock. An inspection of that offered by Mr. Jewell B. Williams, doing business in Fort Fairfield will go far to explain the wide popularity of his establishment, for it is certainly varied enough to enable all tastes to be suited, while the prices are low enough to suit the most economically disposed. The assortment includes clothing, boots, shoes, hats, caps, etc., of every description, and is so frequently renewed as always to be fresh and attractive. Mr. Williams is a native of Houlton, Me., and succeeded to the entire management of the business in 1885, it having been originally founded by Mr. B. J. Stevens many years ago. Employment is given to four assistants, and callers are assured prompt and polite attention, every opportunity being given to make intelligent and satisfactory choice from the heavy stock carried. Mr. Williams also runs a livery stable, having accommodations for thirty horses. Those wishing to hire a first-class team will find such at his stable, which can be obtained at very moderate prices.

N. H. MARTIN, dealer in Cigars, Tobacco, Pipes and Smokers' Articles, Nuts, Fruit, Confections, and Fancy Groceries; Restaurant in connection; Fort Fairfield, Me.—There is, perhaps, no kind of information more constantly in demand than that relating to confections, fruit, tobacco, etc., for everybody wants to know where a satisfactory assortment of goods included in this line of business may be had at a reasonable price, and such questions are much more easily asked than answered. However, we think that we are in a position to give the address of at least one establishment which can hardly fail to give satisfaction to our readers, and that is the one located at Fort Fairfield. This popular enterprise was inaugurated in 1890 by Mr. C. F. Ross, and sold to N. H. Martin in 1891. The intelligent and highly efficient management of the proprietor has decidedly gained a popularity for this house, and it now ranks with the most satisfactorily conducted institutions of the kind in this town. The premises occupied comprise, in addition to a store, a confectionery restaurant capable of accommodating twenty-eight guests. Employment is given to four assistants, and all patrons are served promptly as well as politely. Mr. Martin does an extensive wholesale and retail business, and carries a fresh and desirable assortment of nuts, fruits, confections and fancy groceries, as well as the best brands of cigars, tobacco, pipes and smokers' articles in general. Low prices prevail in all departments of the establishment, and the wishes of patrons are most carefully studied in every respect.

A. B. DEARBORN, General Commission Agent, Lumber and Potatoes, Fort Fairfield, Me.—The enterprise carried on by Mr. A. B. Dearborn may be divided into two departments, or perhaps it would be more nearly correct to say that he carries on two distinct enterprises for they have but little connection, although one doubtless helps the other. He is a general commission agent, making a specialty of lumber and potatoes and being prepared to furnish either or both in very large quantities at short notice, and is also a grocer, carrying a well-chosen and complete stock and selling at retail at the lowest market rates. Mr. Dearborn was born in Corinna, Me., and has been identified with his present undertakings since 1884, during which time he has established a most enviable reputation for fair dealing, promptness and accuracy in the filling of orders and has become very favorably known among both producers and consumers. He is prepared to execute extensive commissions for the furnishing of lumber or potatoes to the best possible advantage, and all communications will be given immediate and careful attention. Mr. Dearborn prepares one of the very best condition powders for horses known to the world. It is an old English preparation and is very much sought after. Mr. Dearborn is selling large quantities of it.

ALFRED A. HOCKENHULL, Grist Mill, Fort Fairfield, Me.—Machinery will do a great deal but it will not do everything; that is to say, even the most improved and perfect machinery will not long do good work unless it is properly used and adjusted, and many of our readers know from experience that it is not so much the mill as the miller that ensures good results. The grist mill carried on by Mr. Alfred A. Hockenhull, and located about one-half of a mile from the village, is well equipped, but it would never be so popular as it is were not Mr. Hockenhull an expert and practical miller who spares no pains to do strictly first-class work at all times. He is a native of England, and during the year he has carried on his present mill has won a high reputation for skill, promptness in filling orders, and fair dealing with all. Custom grinding is done at short notice and at fair rates, and grain and mill feed will be furnished in quantities to suit, bottom prices being quoted on articles of standard merit. Mr. Hockenhull has at great expense built a fine dam at his mill which gives him an excellent water power the year around.

A. M. EARLE,

UNDERTAKER,

FORT FAIRFIELD. ME.

A FULL SUPPLY OF FUNERAL GOODS CONSTANTLY ON HAND.

All Orders will receive prompt attention.

JOS. S. HALL, Dealer in Hardware, Paints and Oils, Doors, Windows, etc., Fort Fairfield, Me.—The enterprise now conducted by Mr. Jos. S. Hall, was founded in 1885, he having formerly been a blacksmith, and also dealt in iron, etc. He is a native of Searsport, Me., and is very well known throughout the business circles of Fort Fairfield. The premises utilized by him comprise a store 24×34 feet in dimensions, in addition to a storehouse 24×40 feet in size, which are fully occupied by the varied and heavy stock constantly carried. Among the more important articles dealt in may be mentioned hardware, paints, oils, doors, windows, etc., and no house in this section is in a position to offer more genuine inducements to buyers than the one under consideration. Retail purchasers are not generally expert judges of the articles they wish to procure, and hence are peculiarly liable to imposition. To such we would say buy of a reliable house, such a one as that conducted by Mr. Hall, for this house has an unblemished reputation, and then you may feel assured of perfectly honorable treatment, and of getting an article that is bound to suit. No fancy prices are quoted, full value being returned for every dollar received in every instance. Orders can be filled at very short notice when necessary.

JOSEPH B. ROBBINS, Manufacturer of Starch and Potato Barrels, Fort Fairfield, Me.—Regarded from any point of view, the enterprise conducted by Mr. Joseph B. Robbins, in Fort Fairfield, is one of great importance, and it must be evident to any observer that it could never have attained its present magnitude had it not been most skillfully and intelligently managed. Mr. Robbins is a native of Knox county, Me. He began business in Fort Fairfield a few years ago, and is now one of our best known business men in town, and is highly esteemed for his reliable business methods and his readiness to do all in his power to advance the interests of this section. The premises occupied are conveniently fitted with every requisite facility, and an extensive business is done in the manufacture of starch and potato barrels, employment is constantly given to six thoroughly competent workmen. While quickly responding to every call of his customers Mr. Robbins assures all that he only makes such barrels as will prove their value in actual service, for he has had sufficient experience to know that many an appliance which looks well "on paper," utterly fails to give satisfaction when put to actual service. His prices are as low as the use of first-class materials and the employment of skilled labor will allow, and orders for any quantity of barrels will be promptly filled.

AMASA HOWE, Shingle Mill, Fort Fairfield, Me.—The introduction of machinery has worked wonderful changes in many industries but in no case has more change been made than in the manufacture of shingles, for by the old method they were slowly and laboriously made by hand by the carpenters who were building the house they were to cover, while now they are turned out with almost magical rapidity by machinery, and a carpenter would no more think of making a shingle by hand than he would of cutting off a joist with a jack-knife. Shingle machines have been greatly improved since they were first brought out and a mill equipped with the most improved machinery can produce shingles at surprisingly low rates; so it is not surprising that Mr. Amasa Howe should be able to quote bottom prices on shingles for his mill is thoroughly well equipped, being fitted up with a complete plant of the most improved machinery, driven by steam power. Its capacity is large, employment is given to twenty assistants, and even the heaviest orders can be filled at very short notice. Mr. Howe is a resident of Presque Isle, Me., and is very widely known in this section, having built up a very extensive business since beginning operations some six years ago.

JAMES B. GREY, Blacksmithing and Job Work, Fort Fairfield, Me.—Mr. James B. Grey is a native of Caribou, Me., and has long been identified with the blacksmith's trade, being known as one of the most expert blacksmiths in Fort Fairfield. Since he opened his shop in 1884, he has materially added to both his reputation and his business, for his improved facilities enable him to fill every order without long delay, and to do work cheaply as well as durably and neatly. The premises made use of are some 1,064 square feet in dimensions, and are thoroughly equipped in every part, especially as regards the facilities of blacksmithing and job work, of which a specialty is made. Mr. Grey builds small boiler engines, and gives especial attention to repairing machinery, threshing machines, horse powers, mowing machines, horse rakes, engines, boilers, guns and revolvers repaired neatly and well. Traps and springs of all kinds made and repaired. Keys made and fitted for locks of all descriptions. Taps and dies repaired, and is prepared to do such work in a manner that will suit his customers. The prices quoted in various departments of the business are as low as is consistent with the use of selected material, and the employment of skilled labor, and we may say in closing that all work done at this establishment is fully warranted in every respect, being done at very reasonable prices, and in the best manner possible.

A. C. CARY, dealer in Dry Goods, Boots and Shoes, Groceries and General Merchandise, Fort Fairfield, Me.—Every old established business enterprise has a character of its own, which is as sharply defined and as generally known as is that of a prominent public man, and our well-informed Fort Fairfield readers will agree that the main characteristic of the undertaking carried on by Mr. A. C. Cary is reliability, for the policy of this gentleman has ever been to keep faith with the public, and as a natural consequence, the public put implicit confidence in the announcements and methods of this house. The business was founded in 1860 by A. C. Cary, and so conducted until 1870, when the firm name was changed to A. C. & L. K. Cary. In 1871 Mr. A. C. Cary, the present proprietor, again assumed full control of the business, it thus being one of the oldest as well as one of the best known enterprises of the kind in this town. Spacious and well-equipped premises are utilized, and a very heavy and skillfully chosen stock of general merchandise is carried, comprising dry goods, boots and shoes, groceries, etc., they being selected with an eye to the requirements of the best trade, and being renewed so frequently as always to include the very latest fashionable novelties. Employment is given to two competent assistants, and callers may depend upon receiving immediate and courteous attention, and upon having goods represented to them precisely as they are, for, as we have before stated, this house is noted for fair and honorable dealing, and the most inexperienced buyer may depend upon getting full value for every dollar expended, especially as the lowest market rates are quoted on all the goods dealt in. Mr. Cary is a native of Turner, Me., and is well known throughout Fort Fairfield, where he has held the office of selectman, and is now postmaster.

L. K. CARY & CO., Established in 1871, Dealers in Hardware, Farm Machinery, Crockery, Glass and Silverware, Builders' Material, Plumbers' Supplies, Stoves and Tin Ware, Fort Fairfield, Me.—The establishment now conducted by Mr. L. K. Cary & Co., was founded in 1871, and has been under the management of the present firm since 1886. They have built up a very extensive business and attained the most favorable relations with manufacturers of farm machinery, builders' material, plumbers' supplies, etc., the consequence being that it is prepared to furnish any and all of those commodities at bottom prices and to fill the most extensive orders at short notice. The partners are Messrs. L. K. Cary and E. L. Houghton, both being natives of Maine. One floor and a basement, each measuring 40×136 feet, are utilized, so that a heavy stock can be and is constantly carried, including in addition to farm machinery, builders' material and plumbers' supplies, full lines of crockery, glass and silver ware, also stoves, tin ware, etc. These goods being fully warranted, and being furnished at as low rates as are quoted on any first-class goods. The bulk of the business is retail, and as employment is given to three assistants all orders are assured immediate and careful attention.

J. F. HACKER, Dry Goods and Groceries, Fort Fairfield, Me.—In Fort Fairfield, as in any community, it is necessary to have considerable knowledge of the different mercantile concerns in order to buy to the best advantage, but those who are wise enough to profit by the experience of others do not need to live long in a place in order to learn where and how to get the best value for their money, and those who will visit Mr. J. F. Hacker's establishment when they want anything in the line of dry goods, groceries, etc., will do as well as they could if they had lived in Fort Fairfield all their lives, for at no store in this town is a more liberal policy followed, or lower prices quoted. Mr. Hacker is a native of Lee, Me., and is very widely known in Fort Fairfield, where he has held the

office of town treasurer. The business now carried on by him was originally founded by Mr. Isaac Hacker in 1860, and after two or three changes in its management came into the sole possession of the present proprietor in 1887. The store occupied covers an area of 30×75 feet, being very attractive in appearance. The trade is retail and the stock is correspondingly large and varied, it always including full lines of dry goods, boots and shoes, and groceries, the leading novelties, as well as staple goods being offered in both departments. Employment is given to five efficient assistants, and customers are served promptly and politely, every article sold by this house being guaranteed to prove just as represented in every respect.

COLLINS HOUSE, M. E. Collins, Proprietor, Fort Fairfield, Me.—The Collins House is one of the best known hotels in Aroostook county, for it was originally opened by Mr. H. C. Collins in 1878, he being succeeded in 1884 by F. P. Collins, and he in 1889 by the present proprietor, M. E. Collins. It has been excellently managed from the start, each proprietor having looked after the details of the business with such fidelity as to maintain the high reputation of the house so long enjoyed. The Collins House is a thoroughly comfortable hotel, it is homelike and is the place that many traveling men make it a point to reach and remain over Sunday. The house contains forty sleeping-rooms and these are pleasant and comfortably furnished and neatly kept. The table is supplied with an abundance of seasonable and substantial food, neatly served and the guests are not obliged to wait long before they are attended to, as eight assistants are employed and the service is prompt and efficient. The terms of the house are reasonable and it thoroughly deserves the patronage of all appreciative of good accommodations and liberal methods. A good livery, feed and sale stable is connected with the house containing twenty stalls and is fitted up with all conveniences for the comfort of horses, while first-class teams may be obtained at reasonable rates. In conclusion, we would advise strangers coming to Fort Fairfield, to stop at the Collins House feeling assured that they will carry away pleasant remembrances of their stay at this hotel. The proprietor is ably seconded by the genial and obliging clerk (Danny), Mr. D. W. Vanwart, and the fine old gentleman, Mr. Slocomb, who always has a kind word for everyone.

W. W. SLOCOMB & CO., successors to M. Schmuckler & Co., dealers in Clothing, Gents' Furnishings, Boots and Shoes, Fort Fairfield, Me.—Those who have made a trial of the clothing supplied by Messrs. W. W. Slocomb & Co., of this town are already conversant with its merits, and need no persuasion from us to induce them to favor this firm with their patronage, but as our book will be read by many who have not yet had business relations with them, we feel that the space at our disposal can be occupied in no better way than by a brief consideration of some of the advantages they are prepared to offer their customers. Those who want wearing apparel at once, or who for any reason prefer ready-made clothing, can have their wants attended to at this establishment, and can feel assured that they are being used as well as they could be anywhere, both as regards the desirability of the clothing, and the prices named on the same. A fine assortment of clothing, gent's furnishings, and boots and shoes are constantly on hand, enabling a wide latitude of choice to be had in the selection of goods. The premises occupied cover an area of 1260 square feet. A sufficient force of help is employed to attend to the wants of all the patrons. Mr. Slocomb is a native of Fort Fairfield, and succeeded M. Schmuckler & Co. in his present line of business in 1886. His business is a steadily growing one and no efforts are spared to make every customer a permanent one. All articles dealt in are warranted according to the prices, which will not fail to give satisfaction.

C. D. CUTTS, dealer in Hardware, Cutlery, Doors, Sash and Blinds ; Agent for the celebrated Golden Clarion Range ; special attention given to Pipe Fitting, Plumbing and Hot Water Heating ; Fort Fairfield, Me.—The establishment now conducted by Mr. C. D. Cutts is one of the most popular of its kind in this vicinity, and, indeed, will compare favorably as regards variety and desirability of the stock on hand with many of the leading hardware stores in the larger cities. The premises occupied are two stores and basements 24 × 60 and 30 × 60, connected by arches. These are located in the new block erected by Mr. Cutts, and this space is fully availed of in the accommodation of the immense stock carried, and the extensive business done, which consists of manufacturing and dealing at both wholesale and retail, in stoves, furnaces, pumps and tinware, etc. The block is one of the finest in this section of the State. It is 75 × 60 feet in size and three stories in height. A Morse improved freight and passenger elevator runs to the upper floors. The stores have French plate glass windows and are very handsomely fitted up. Business was founded in 1879 by Messrs. Cutts & Gray, the present proprietor, Mr. C. D. Cutts assuming full control in 1880. He is a native of Gardiner, Me., and is very well known throughout Fort Fairfield and vicinity. Employment is given to efficient assistants, and orders for pipe fitting, plumbing and hot water heating, furnace and stove work are assured immediate and skillful attention. Mr. Cutts is agent for the "Golden Clarion Range," and deals in cutlery, hardware, doors, sash and blinds, also agricultural implements, wind mills, dairy supplies, sanitary earthenware, paints, oils, varnishes, crockery, glass and wooden ware. The charges made in all departments of the business being uniformly moderate for first class work and strictly reliable goods.

———

A. C. PAUL, Dealer in Books, Fine Stationery, Blank Books and School Supplies, Best Inks, Mucilage, etc. ; Window Shades and Draperies, Curtain Fixtures and Drapery Poles, Room Papers and Ceiling Decorations in great variety. Ladies' and Children's Furnishing Goods, Fancy Goods and Circulating Library, etc., etc., Main Street, Fort Fairfield, Me.—The business now conducted by A. C. Paul was originally started by Mr. F. H. Chase about fifteen years ago, he being succeeded by the present proprietress in 1881. Mrs. Paul was born in Fort Fairfield and therefore needs no introduction to a large proportion of our readers for no dealer in town is more generally known, and we may add, more highly esteemed. The premises utilized are conveniently located on Main street and cover an area of some 2000 square feet where is carried a large stock of books, fine stationery, blank books, and school supplies, best inks, mucilage, etc., as well as window shades and draperies, curtain fixtures, and drapery poles, room papers and ceiling decorations in great variety, while ladies' and childrens' furnishing goods, fancy goods, etc., etc., are also offered at the lowest prices. Mrs. Paul conducts a fine circulating library where good and popular books are let on very reasonable terms. Mrs. Paul pursues but one policy regarding the goods she handles, her aim being to give the largest possible return for money received. This may seem incredible to those who believe in selling at as high a figure as possible, but Mrs. Paul's long experience has no doubt taught her that the public appreciate liberal methods and at all events no establishment in this town is more highly and deservedly popular. Employment is given to careful and attentive assistants, and all patrons are promptly as well as politely served. Mrs. Paul has for years been local correspondent for several newspapers, and in May, 1891, was appointed by Governor Burleigh as one of the board of World's Fair managers of Maine.

CUTTS & SCATES FURNITURE CO., Fort Fairfield, Me.—Parties who are contemplating housekeeping, or who wish to replenish their houses for the coming winter with elegant and durable furniture and carpets, will be gratified to learn of the recently formed "Cutts & Scates Furniture Co." This is made up of the enterprising houses of C. D. Cutts and Scates & Co., and the premises occupied in the new Cutts block will be found very attractive and well adapted for the display of the large stock of new and beautiful goods, embracing the latest styles of parlor and chamber sets, rattan goods, mirrors and draperies, which are sold both at wholesale and retail, and on very favorable terms. The two floors occupied are each 60×75 feet, and an elegantly fitted-up office is occupied on the ground-floor. The advantage of purchasing of this firm is obvious as their stock is not only new and fresh, but it is bought in car load lots from the factory, the putting together, decorating and painting being done here by the best of skilled labor. They also make a specialty of the manufacture of mattresses in all grades from excelsior to hair, and upholstering is a leading feature of the business, also. As the stock now displayed is one of the largest and most varied ever offered in this section of the State it would be well for all housekeepers to visit the warerooms, access to which is gained by an elevator from the street floor. If the success attained by the proprietors in their other stores is any indication we predict for them an immense trade.

———

THOS. WINTER, Tailor ; Fort Fairfield, Me.—It is all very well to say "everyone should dress well," but the fact remains that everyone does not know how to dress well, for taste in dress is by no means general, or even a common gift, and those who have no taste in this direction do not always know where they can get competent or dependable advice. In this connection we take pleasure in calling attention to the establishment conducted by Mr. Thos. Winter, and located at Fort Fairfield. Mr. Winter is a native of England, and has been identified with his present line of business in this town since 1889. This gentleman is a merchant tailor of experience and ability, and as he has both taste and skill in his chosen line of work, those who feel uncertain as to what they should wear, should certainly give him a call, for he will cheerfully give advice when desired, and he is fully prepared to carry that advice into practical effect, and to guarantee satisfaction to his patrons. Orders can be filled at short notice, and those who wish a stylish, good fitting and honestly made suit, or garment, at a moderate price, can get just what they desire at this well-known establishment.

———

H. N. GOODHUE, wholesale and retail Grocer ; Teas, Coffees, Flour, Tobacco ; Fort Fairfield, Me.—The wonderful advance made in transportation facilities during the past half century has had the effect of placing the productions of the whole world at the command of every civilized nation, and, therefore, has very largely increased the number of articles coming under the head of "groceries," the result being that but comparatively few dealers carry a really complete line of such goods. Mr. H. N. Goodhue may be cited as a prominent exception to the rule, however, for he enters very energetically and intelligently to all classes of trade, utilizing premises comprising a store and basement each 3,600 square feet, in addition to a storehouse 1,728 square feet in size, and offers an assortment of staple and fancy groceries, flour, teas, coffees, tobacco, etc., which bear evidence of very careful selection, and which is exceptionally complete in every department. Mr. Goodhue is a native of Bangor, Me. He has been identified with the grocery business in Fort Fairfield since 1880. He enjoys the most favorable relations with producers, and is thoroughly well qualified to meet all honorable competition, both as regards the quality of the goods handled and the prices quoted on the same. Mr. Goodhue does both a wholesale and retail business, and is prepared to fill orders without delay, employment being given to five assistants. This store is provided with a cyclone coffee mill run by water power, which enables Mr. Goodhue to easily handle a large coffee trade. A fine large refrigerator with roll top glass front and plate glass mirror, adds much to the appearance of his place which has gained the reputation of being the finest grocery north of Bangor. Mr. Goodhue is well known in this vicinity, having held the office of town clerk for several years.

E. J. DORSEY, Livery, Board, Feed and Sale Stable, Fort Fairfield, Me.—Considering that it is almost impossible to find two men who will agree on all points as to what constitutes a good horse, it is not at all strange that no livery stable keeper has ever lived who perfectly satisfied everybody, but of course there is a good deal of difference observable in the methods practiced at the various public stables, and as we wish our readers to go where they will be assured prompt and polite attention, and thoroughly first-class service in every respect, we take pleasure in calling their favorable attention to the establishment now conducted by Mr. E. J. Dorsey, for this is one of the best equipped livery, boarding, feed and sale stables in Fort Fairfie'd, and the management is liberal, enterprising and reliable. This establishment was founded in 1884 by Messrs. Dorsey Brothers and came into the possession of the present proprietor in 1886. Mr. E. J. Dorsey is a native of Fort Fairfield, and his thorough

experience gives reason for trusting the most valuable horses to his care. His stable is spacious and well arranged and in addition to a carriage room, contains twenty eight stalls. Horses will be taken to board, and assured the best of care and an abundance of proper food. Some excellent teams are available for livery purposes, and the charges made are uniformly moderate. Horses for sale will be shown to their best advantage and to the satisfaction of their owners.

H. O. PERRY, Agent for Life, Fire and Accident Insurance, Fort Fairfield, Me.—Those familiar with the principles on which insurance is founded need not be told that the cost of insurance to the insured is to a great extent beyond the control of the companies furnishing it, nor need they be informed that no company and no agent of one or several companies, can furnish *bona-fide* insurance at rates appreciably below those prevailing when the contract of insurance is made. But it would be absurd to conclude from this that it is of no special consequence how or by whom you are insured, for some companies are thoroughly reliable while others are, to say the least, "uncertain," and some agencies afford a very prompt and accurate service, while others are conducted on a sort of "go-as-you-please" plan not calculated to inspire confidence. Hence we take pleasure in calling attention to the Fire, Life and Accident Insurance office of Mr. H. O. Perry, first, because this gentleman represents some of the leading companies; and second, because the service they render is unsurpassed whether as regards promptness or entire reliability. Mr. Perry founded his business in Blane, Me., in 1867, and has been located in Fort Fairfield since 1875. He was born in Richmond, Me., and is well and favorably known in both business and social circles. Mr. Perry gives attention to all commissions and represents the following thoroughly reliable companies: Home, New York; American, New York; Niagara, New York; Mechanics and Traders', New York; Orient, Hartford, Conn.; British America, Toronto, Ca.; Insurance Company of North America, Philadelphia; Bangor Mutual, Bangor, Me

HISTORICAL SKETCH OF DANFORTH, ME.

There are but three townships in the Fourth Range north of Bingham's Purchase that have developed sufficiently to have b come of any special importance, and each of these is intersected by the Maine Central railway and possesses natural advantages which fully account for the prosperity of the town controlling them. Mattawamkeag, Kingman and Danforth are the names of the towns in question, the first two lying side by side, and being separated by Drew plantation and Township No. 8 from Danforth, which is in Washington county, while Mattawamkeag and Kingman are in Penobscot county.

Danforth is by far the largest of the three towns and indeed is one of the largest in the State, its area being about equal to that of the two others combined. The township lies in the extreme north of Washington county, it being bounded on the north by Bancroft and Weston in Aroostook county and by Schoodic Grand Lake, which also partially bounds it on the east, the rest of the eastern boundary being furnished by Forest City. Danforth is bounded on the south by Township No. 9, Third Range, and on the west by Township No. 8 of the Fourth Range. The northern boundary line is about nine miles long but the average breadth of the township is more than ten and one-half miles, the southern boundary line being eleven miles in length. The western boundary line is six miles long and the line dividing Danforth from Forest City, on the east is about four miles long. The township is oblong in shape and is regular in outline with the exception of its northwestern corner, this bordering upon Grand Lake and being very uneven.

There are no very large or important lakes or ponds entirely within the town, or rather there is none of natural origin, for the long pond which lies above the mills at Danforth village was made by damming the outlet of Baskahegan Lake, which lies in the adjoining township The water privilege at the village is one of the best in the entire State and is unquestionably destined to prove a powerful factor in the future development of the town, for although manufacturing has been quite largely carried on here for years but a small fraction of the available power is utilized, and a more favorable opening for the establishment of a manufacturing plant cannot be found in Maine, rich as the State is in such opportunities.

The dam at the village has recently been rebuilt, and under present conditions the most prolonged "dry spell" would have no appreciable effect upon the mill-pond, which is exceptionally large, it extending fully six miles above the mills. It is fed by two large lakes, the Jackson Brook and the Baskahegan. The latter is the more important of the two and is a noble body of water, some six and one-half miles long and from three to seven miles in width. It occupies the greater part of the unnamed township south of Danforth and a large portion of it extends over into Township 6 of the Second Range. The Baskahegan lies six miles above the mill-pond and twelve miles above the mills, and has a good dam across its mouth. It holds an enormous amount of water, so large in fact that even under the most unfavorable circumstances there is no lack of the quantity required for all mill or factory purposes. On the dam at Danforth village are located a grist mill and a saw mill,— and a hint concerning Danforth's advantages and the possibilities of this location is afforded by the fact that at the grist mill is ground a large amount of corn shipped direct from the West at a very low rate of freight. Other grains are also extensively ground at this establishment. The saw mill produces more than three million feet of long lumber during the season, besides turning out three million laths and about a million and a half shingles.

Despite the magnitude of both these mills there is a very large amount of unused power here and this is certainly an excellent location for a factory, especially as the owners of the water privilege are ready and willing to meet responsible parties half-way, and to offer substantial inducements for them to come and put in a factory thoroughly equipped with modern machinery. Not only the owners of the privilege but the community in general appreciate the benefits arising from the operations of a first-class factory, and as the residents of the town are as liberal and enterprising as they are intelligent there is no doubt that such a factory would be made exempt from taxation for a term of years. This chance is well worthy of investigation, and prompt action in the matter is advisable for the opportunity is far too favorable to long remain unimproved.

There are other important commodities beside flour, meal, feed, and long and short lumber manufactured in the town, among these being carriages, last blocks, jewelry, harnesses, smith work, machine work, drugs and patent medicines.

Danforth was incorporated March 17, 1860, but the first settlement within the township took place long before that date, it being made in 1829 by Parker Tewksbury, of Cornville ; and a few years later Eliphalet Morse, Nathaniel Schillinger and Jeremiah Schillinger, from Poland, Joseph Webber, from Clinton, and Seth Stinchfield, from Leeds, came to town. The early growth of Danforth was by no means remarkable for its rapidity, more than thirty years elapsing before a population of 300 was attained; the census of 1860 giving the town a population of 280, and even after incorporation the development was very slow, the gain in ten years ending in 1870, being but 33 so far as population was concerned. But the next decade witnessed a remarkable change in the rate of growth, the population increasing nearly 100 per cent, or from 313 to 612. Decided gain was also made from 1880 to 1890, the population by the last census being 1063, and the estate valuation being $179,055 as compared with $106,934 in 1880. A good part of this increase however was caused by the annexation of a part of Weston, in 1885, and of a part Eaton, in 1887.

The Maine Central R. R., runs entirely across the town from to north to south, making stations at Danforth and Eaton Villages which are five miles apart. The bulk of the population, business, etc., is at Danforth Village where there are many fine stores, good hotels and well-equipped manufacturing establishments. The local associations include lodges of Masons and Odd Fellows and a society of the Ancient Order of United Workmen ; together with the Danforth Band, Danforth Trotting Park Association, and the Union Hall Corporation. Danforth has an industrious and intelligent population among whom are many public-spirited business men who have full confidence in the extensive future development of the town and spare neither trouble nor expense to hasten it by every means in their power.

DANFORTH MILLS.

Representative Business Men of Danforth, Me.

HATHORN, FOSS & CO. (Mills at Danforth, Lambert Lake, La Grange, Alton.) manufacturers of Foreign and Domestic fruit Box Shooks, Long Lumber, Staves, Shingles, Spool Stock, Back-board, etc., Danforth, Me.—The student of Maine's history cannot help being very forcibly impressed by the great enterprise the residents of the State have always shown in finding a market for their productions, for they have pushed their operations in every quarter of the globe and for many years Maine was the leading commercial State in the Union and would be such to-day were it not for the decline of American shipping Spars from the forests of Maine were shipped to all the leading maritime nations so long as the supply lasted; cooperage stock has been largely exported for many years; Maine ice was the first to be shipped from one State or one country to another; Maine canned goods rule the market, Maine starch is almost universally known and used; Maine lumber has for years held a leading position in the market,—in short our citizens have been most active in developing the State's resources, and a firm which has a most honorable record in that respect is that of Hathorn, Foss & Co., which carries on mills at Danforth, Lambert Lake, La Grange and Alton, and is very extensively engaged in the manufacture of foreign and domestic fruit box shooks, long lumber, staves, shingles, spool stock, back-board, etc. Employment is given to from 150 to 250 assistants, and the mills are fitted up with improved machinery driven by steam power, the total product being very large and a great proportion of it being shipped to Southern Europe, as the concern are in a position to compete successfully with any other house in the world in the production of fruit box shooks, etc. As now constituted, the firm is made up of Messrs. Obed Foss, Russell Bennett, and Allen Hackett, all of whom are natives of Maine, Messrs. Foss and Hackett having been born in Pittsfield, and Mr. Bennett in Palmyra. These gentlemen are very widely known in business circles and are doing much to develop this section of the State. The firm opened a general store in Danforth, in 1884, and carry a very large and complete stock of reliable goods which are sold at the very lowest market rates.

JOHN A. WEATHERBEE & CO., Successors to Weatherbee, Bubar & Co., manufacturers and dealers in Long and Short Lumber, Shingles, Laths and Pickets ; Custom Sawing also done ; Office at J. A. Weatherbee's Store ; Danforth, Me.—The firm of John A. Weatherbee & Co. was formed in 1889, and succeeded Messrs. Weatherbee, Bubar & Co., who, in 1885, had succeeded Messrs. Goodwin Brothers, the last named firm having succeeded Messrs. Dodge & Goodwin in 1879. The present concern is made up of Messrs. J. A. Weatherbee and Chas. E. Berry, both of whom are natives of Springfield, Me., and have long ranked with the most prominent business men of this section. Mr. Weatherbee has served as selectman, and Mr. Berry as town clerk, and both are almost universally known in social as well as in business circles. They are manufacturers of and dealers in long and short lumber, shingles, laths, pickets, etc., and are prepared to fill the largest orders at short notice and at bottom rates. Employment is given to some thirty assistants, and custom sawing will be done promptly, accurately and at moderate figures. The office is at Mr. J. A. Weatherbee's store, which contains a large and very carefully chosen stock of general merchandise, and has been carried on by him for about twelve years. Reliable goods, low prices and prompt service have had their usual effect, and this store is largely patronized and considered as representative in every sense of the word.

A. McCLAIN, Jr., Gents' Furnishing Goods ; Ready made Clothing ; Danforth, Me.—One need not be very old to be able to remember when ready-made clothing was worn only by those who could not afford custom garments, for it was poorly made, ill-fitting and unfashionable in cut, but this is all changed nowadays, and by patronizing a reliable and enterprising house, you may obtain clothing that cannot be distinguished from custom work, while its cost is very much less. The establishment carried on by Mr. A. McClain, Jr., is a prime favorite with those who appreciate first-class clothing, and there is every reason why it should be, for one may always find here a large and complete assortment of seasonable garments, including the very latest fashionable novelties, while the prices are remarkably low and the goods are in every instance guaranteed to prove as represented. Mr. McClain is a native of this State, and holds the position of town clerk in Danforth. He is universally and favorably known throughout this section. He gives careful personal attention to customers, and, as employment is given to competent assistants, the service is prompt, accurate and obliging at all times. The store occupied is 22×30 feet in dimensions, and contains not only clothing of all kinds, but also a well chosen stock of gents' furnishing goods, the styles being correct and the prices as low as the lowest, and suitable for all tastes and purses.

THE EXCHANGE, Three Minutes' Walk from Station, R. B. Stinchfield, Proprietor, Danforth, Me.—The pretentious and absurd claims, which are made in behalf of some hotels have done much to make the public, and especially the travelling public, look with suspicion on any house which is asserted to be decidedly superior to the average, and therefore we feel placed in a somewhat embarrassing position as regards "The Exchange Hotel," for any mention of it, which will do it justice, must make it appear decidedly superior to the majority of public houses carried on under similar conditions. Some people are extremely hard to suit, and even the most efficient service does not give them entire satisfaction but we have yet to hear a complaint of the accommodations or the management of The Exchange Hotel, the unanimous verdict being that it is a thoroughly comfortable and homelike hostelry, that guests are assured prompt and polite service, and that the terms are remarkably low considering the accommodations provided. Now this of course is high praise, but it comes from competent and unprejudiced judges, and is consequently worthy of careful consideration. The present proprietor, Mr. R. B. Stinchfield is a native of this town and took its management in 1886. He gives close personal attention to the supervision of affairs and employs four competent assistants. The hotel can accommodate twenty guests, and the rooms are comfortably furnished and kept in neat and trim condition at all times. There is a first class livery connected with the house and teams will be furnished at short notice and at moderate rates. The hotel is pleasantly situated being only three minutes walk from railroad depot, and special rates are made to travelling men. Since Mr. Stinchfield took the agency of the celebrated Estey organ and pianos, the travelling salesmen for musical instruments find it unnecessary to put in an appearance with any other makes for they all call for Estey.

B. F. RUNNELLS, dealer in Dry and Fancy Goods, Boots and Shoes, Groceries and General Merchandise, Danforth, Me.—Probably one of the best-known establishments of the kind in this town is that conducted by Mr. B. F. Runnells, for this enterprise was inaugurated in 1872. The present proprietor is a native Marrion, Me., and has become thoroughly identified with the undertaking in question. The premises utilized comprise one store 24×32 feet, together with a wing 20×26 feet in dimensions, and a stock is constantly on hand to choose from, it being made up of dry and fancy goods, stationery, confectionery, groceries, boots and shoes, fruit, etc., etc., and many other commodities too numerous to mention. Mr. Runnells caters to no special class of trade, but strives to offer a sufficient variety of goods to suit all tastes and purses, and to quote positively the lowest market rates at all times. He has built up an extensive business during his long and honorable career, and has an unsurpassed reputation for selling goods strictly on their merits, no misrepresentation being practiced under any circumstances. Mr. Runnells has held the position of town clerk and been a selectman of Danforth. Orders are filled promptly, and courteous attention assured all callers.

DANFORTH DRUG STORE, Drugs and Medicines, Toilet Soaps, Perfumery, Brushes, Sponges, and all kinds of Druggists' Sundries usually kept in a first-class drug store; Prescriptions and Family Recipes carefully compounded; Danforth, Me.—It would be difficult to find an establishment of more genuine value to the community than that carried on by Dr. M. L. Porter of the "Danforth Drug Store." This enterprise was founded in 1885, and has been under the able management of its present proprietor, and has largely developed as its influence to the public became more plainly manifest. Drugs and medicines are supplied at retail at the lowest rates that can be named on first class goods, and, as prescriptions and family recipes are carefully compounded, customers may feel assured of their favors being appreciated and their orders being handled with that skill and accuracy so desirable in this connection. Every precaution is observed that will tend to reduce the liability of error to the smallest possible amount, and every facility is at hand that can aid in attaining this result. Dr. Porter is moderate in his charges and certainly has solved the problem of combining reliable service with popular prices. The sale of toilet soaps, perfumery, brushes, sponges and all kinds of druggists' sundries usually kept in a first class drug store forms another important department of his business, and is conducted on the same liberal scale that characterizes the management of his drug trade. The stock carried is fresh, warranted genuine, and of the best quality. Dr. Porter is a native of Bangor, Me., and is favorably known as an upright and enterprising business man.

W. S. ELLIS, dealer in Dry and Fancy Goods, Groceries, Glassware, Lamps, Confectionery, Tobacco and Cigars, Danforth, Me.—The store occupied by Mr. W. S. Ellis is one of the most popular in the town, the stock is complete in every department, and is made up of carefully selected goods which may be confidently relied upon to be precisely as represented. Mr. Ellis is a native of Weston, Me, and has carried on his present enterprise since 1890. The premises in use cover an area of some 400 square feet, and are very conveniently fitted up, enabling him to display his goods to excellent advantage, and to handle his goods without confusion or delay. Dry and fancy goods, groceries, glassware, lamps, confectionery, tobacco and cigars, etc., etc., are offered at the very lowest market rates, and all goods are guaranteed to give satisfaction to the most fastidious. Callers are assured prompt and courteous attention and all orders are filled accurately and when promised, and no one who calls at this highly popular establishment will have reason to regret having done so, Mr. Ellis endeavoring to cater to all classes of trade, and to suit all tastes and all purses.

MRS. H. A. HOWARD, Millinery and Fancy Goods, Danforth, Me.—The majority of ladies agree that it is as well to be "out of the world as out of the fashion," and those residing in Danforth or vicinity, have reason to congratulate themselves on the existence of the establishment conducted by Mrs. H. A. Howard, for as long as this continues under its present management there is no reason for being out of the fashion so far as millinery is concerned at least, as here may always be found an assortment comprising the latest novelties in hats, bonnets, and millinery goods in general, together with a varied and carefully chosen stock of fancy goods. Mrs. Howard is a native of Bangor, Me., and has carried on her present enterprise since 1886, having succeeded to the old established business founded many years before by Mrs. L. R. Howard, during the present management a very extensive and desirable patronage has been built up and Mrs Howard has gained an enviable reputation for good taste and business ability. The premises utilized are large and the stock is displayed to excellent advantage, while Mrs. Howard quotes very reasonable prices and spares no pains to fully satisfy every customer.

J. H. SARGENT,

MANUFACTURER OF

CARRIAGES AND WAGONS

Repairing, Painting and Picture Frames a Specialty.

ALL WORK PROMPTLY ATTENDED TO.

ALSO DEALER IN

ALL KINDS OF PAINTS. OILS, GLASS, ETC., ETC.

DANFORTH, MAINE.

GEORGE BUBAR, Proprietor of Grist-Mill, and dealer in Corn, Flour and Feed, Danforth, Me.—As truly representative a business as can be found in this town is that conducted by Mr. George Bubar, for he carries on one of the most important enterprises in town and is conceded on all sides to be the leader in this special line. He is a miller and dealer in all kinds of corn, flour and feed, doing a large retail trade, and prepared to furnish anything in his line in quantities to suit at positively bottom prices. Of course to do this he must have unsurpassed facilities and these he must certainly possess, his establishment being one of the most conveniently arranged of the kind in this vicinity. The premises occupied comprise a store two floors, 40×50 feet in dimensions, together with a grist mill, driven by water power, having the latest type of improved machinery, the meal produced being made from carefully selected material and having a very high reputation in the market. Mr. Bubar, is a native of Brunswick, and the management of this business in 1884 though it had been established many years before by Mr. Jas. H. Dodge, and in addition to his Danforth establishment he carries on a general merchandise store at Orient, Me.

STINCHFIELD & FIFIELD, Plumbers and Sheet Iron Workers, and dealers in Stoves, Furnaces, Tin and Hardware, Pumps, Sinks, Lead Pipe, etc., etc., Danforth, Me.—The importance of the work done by the plumber is so evident that even the least observing cannot fail to appreciate it, partially, at all events, and it is on account of its importance that we feel sure that our readers will be interested in learning of a plumbing establishment which stands second to none in the character of the work done and the fair treatment extended to every customer. We refer to that conducted by Messrs. Stinchfield & Fifield in this town. We feel confident that the closest investigation and most careful trial will only serve to confirm the good opinion which we hold of the enterprise. It was established in 1882 by Mr. G. E. Fifield, who was succeeded by Herbert Goodwin, and in 1888 the present firm took its management, who are plumbers and sheet iron workers, and dealers in stoves, furnaces, tin and hardware, pumps, sinks, lead pipe, etc., etc. The premises occupied consists of two floors 25×40 feet in dimensions, and the firm are prepared to fill all orders with the least possible delay, for they employ only skilled and experienced workmen, and have every facility to aid them in turning out the best of work. Messrs. Stinchfield & Fifield give their close personal attention to the many details of their business, being practical plumbers, and the result of pleasing their customers, is to be seen in the trade carried on.

HOTEL VENDOME, G. E. Davis, Proprietor, situated close by the Depot, Danforth, Me.—Danforth is one of the most attractive towns in Maine, and as it is also quite a business centre, it is visited by many strangers at all seasons of the year. Under these circumstances the question of hotel accommodation assumes no little importance, and it is perfectly safe to assert that the enviable reputation this town enjoys among non-residents is due in a great measure to the nature of the accommodations provided at the Hotel Vendome, for this is a thoroughly well managed establishment, and without making any extravagant pretensions, affords a service decidedly superior to that generally obtainable outside the larger cities. The proprietor, Mr. G. E. Davis, is a native of Dipmont, Me., and has been identified with his present enterprise since 1887. He spares no pains to secure the comfort of guests, and employs an ample force of competent assistants, so that the hotel and its appointments are kept in first class condition, and the service is uniformly prompt and dependable. The Hotel Vendome is situated close by the depot, is a newly built and furnished hotel, containing sixteen sleeping rooms. Meals are served upon the arrival of all trains, while the house is open day and night for the reception and accommodation of its patrons. The terms are very reasonable, and those who stay here once will surely come again.

WHITE COUSINS, Confectioners, and dealers in Tobacco and Cigars, Pipes, Pipe Mounts, Fruits, Nuts, etc.; Job Wagon in connection; Danforth, Me.—The enterprise conducted by Messrs. White Cousins was started by them in 1889. The premises occupied cover an area of some 300 square feet, and are tastefully arranged, and the stock is displayed to good advantage. Confectionery of all kinds is dealt in, and warranted pure and fresh, fruits and nuts in their season are carried in stock, and offered at low prices. Tobacco and cigars, pipes, pipe mounts are also largely dealt in, comprising a good selection to choose from, and at prices that will bear closest comparison with those quoted elsewhere, while all fruits, confections and nuts offered for sale are purchased from the most reliable sources, and are therefore guaranteed to be fresh and of the best to be obtained in the market. W. F. and W. G. White compose the firm of White Cousins, and are natives of Vanceboro, Me., both being well and favorably known in this vicinity, fair in all their dealings with the public, and everything carried in stock by them is warranted to prove just as represented, and the prices will be found to compare favorably with those quoted on similar goods, while courteous attention is given to all callers. In addition to the above business Messrs. Cousins run a job wagon, attending the arrival of all trains, and their prices for trucking or expressing baggage are extremely reasonable.

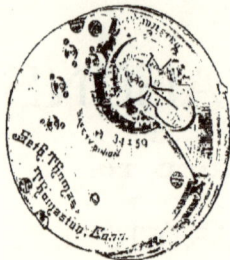

GEORGE CARLTON.

JEWELER AND JOB PRINTER,

Also dealer in Stationery and School Supplies.

Watch repairing a Specialty.

DANFORTH,   -   -   MAINE.

S. W. KIRKPATRICK, Harness Maker, Danforth, Me.—A harness when on a horse properly arranged etc., is a very simple thing in appearance, and apparently is made up of but few parts, but the same harness, when divided up into all the pieces that are combined in its construction, has a very different aspect, and no one can examine it then without feeling, that after all harness making is not the easy thing it may appear to be. Considering the cost of the material and the labor involved to make it up, a first-class harness is sold at a very reasonable figure, and although it is possible to find establishments where fancy figures are charged, still on the whole, most people would prefer to place their order with such a house as that of Mr. S. Kirkpatrick and thus assure themselves a superior article and uniformly fair treatment. This gentleman has carried on his present business for some years and has gained a well earned reputation for the manufacture of fine harness, and the maintenance of moderate prices. Mr. Kirkpatrick is a native of this town and makes light and heavy harness of every description and all kinds of horse furnishings are dealt in and sold at low prices.

H. H. PUTNAM, Groceries, Provisions, Dry Goods, Small Wares, Ready-Made Clothing, Danforth, Me.—The premises utilized by Mr. H. H. Putnam are commodious, occupying two floors 25×60 feet, and a store-house two floors 20×40 feet in dimensions, but they are not too large for the stock carried, anything like detailed mention of his assortment is out of the question, but suffice it to say, it comprises groceries, provisions, dry goods, small wares, ready-made clothing, boots and shoes, hats and caps, wall paper, hardware, paints and oils. Mr. Putnam caters to all classes of trade and his policy of furnishing dependable goods, at bottom prices affords

sufficient explanation of the extent of his business. This enterprise is as truly representative as any to be found in this vicinity it having been inaugurated very many years ago, by Mr. A. I. Hill, he being succeeded in 1874 by the present proprietor, who is a native of Houlton, Me., and served with distinction in the army. He is too well known throughout this section to call for extended personal mention, and we will only add that he spares no pains to maintain the high reputation so long associated with the undertaking with which he is identified.

MRS. A. D. MORSE, Millinery, Dry and Fancy Goods, and Ladies' Boots and Shoes, Danforth, Me.—Such of our readers as are numbered among the fair sex no doubt find the establishment conducted by Mrs. A. D. Morse to be the most attractive in this vicinity, for Mrs. Morse is an extensive dealer in millinery and fancy goods, and always has on hand a very desirable assortment of the latest novelties in these lines. She is a native of this town, and has a large circle of friends here, to which she has added many more since inaugurating her present enterprise in 1890. It would be hardly worth while to attempt to describe a stock which is so constantly changing as is hers, and we will therefore only state that it comprises new millinery, dry and fancy goods, ladies' boots and shoes of various kinds. Mrs. Morse keeps thoroughly well informed concerning the latest dictates of fashion, and the very latest fashionable novelties are obtained as soon as they appear on the market. The store occupied is located in the White Bros. building on Depot street, and is 20×40 feet in dimensions. Mrs. Morse's exceptional taste has given her a most enviable reputation among those who appreciate really artistic millinery effects. She employs several assistants during the busy season, and fills orders at short notice and at moderate rates, besides sparing no pains to show goods.

HISTORICAL SKETCH OF LINCOLN.

Lincoln is remarkable among other towns in this section for its great size, the number of ponds and streams which it contains and which afford abundant and excellent facilities for log driving, the rapidity with which the town developed after its first settlement, its growth in population during 1870–1880, a period when many other Maine towns fell off, and for its excellent railway facilities ; the Maine Central Railway extending along the whole length of its river front, a distance of about ten miles. This is by far the largest town in Penobscot county, it having an area of about 57,000 acres. It is located in about the centre of the central portion of the county and is bounded on the north by the Penobscot River and by Winn ; on the east by Winn and Lee ; on the south by Burlington and Lowell, and on the west by Enfield and the Penobscot River. Its greatest length is eleven miles and its greatest breadth 8½ miles. The surface of the township is uneven and the soil is generally rocky and difficult to cultivate, but along the streams it is much freer from stones and more fertile and some excellent crops are raised. Originally, nearly the entire town was covered by a heavy growth of pine timber but the greater portion has been cleared although there is still some quite valuable timber in the township and an abundant supply of wood. Lumber is largely manufactured as is also spool-stock,—that used for the famous Clark "O. N. T." thread having been made here for years. Tanning is carried on to a considerable extent and there are various other lines of manufacture engaged in, for the excellent water power available has been utilized to a considerable extent from a very early period in the town's history, although its possibilities have not as yet been nearly developed. The ponds and streams wholly or partially within the township are so numerous and important that an adequate description of them would exhaust the entire space at our disposal, and important as is the part they have played in the past development of the town it is but an earnest of what may reasonably be expected of them in the future.

"Cold Stream" would seem to be a favorite name for ponds in this section for besides the large Cold Stream pond in Enfield, there is Little Cold Stream pond in the southwest corner of Lincoln and two Cold Stream ponds east of the former. These ponds and Little Round Pond which lies northeast of them form a chain, they being all connected and emptying finally into the Pissadumkeag River, differing in this respect from the remaining Lincoln ponds, which flow directly into the Penobscot.

The uppermost of these is appropriately named Upper Pond and extends from a point about half a mile north of the Burlington line a mile and a half to the northwest, its average breadth slightly exceeding half a mile. Upper Pond empties into Folsom Pond by an outlet half a mile long, and that pond empties into Mattanawcook Pond by an outlet a mile long whose waters are swelled by the discharge from Crooked Pond which empties into it at a point about midway of its course; Mattanawcook Pond also receives the waters of Dead Stream, and of Rocky Brook.

Another chain of lakes emptying directly into the Penobscot may be found in the northern part of the township, the first one of the series lying three miles northeast of Upper Pond. It is called Caribou Pond and receives the waters of Egg Pond, so-called because its outline resembles that of an egg more or less—but considerably less than more. The next in the chain is Long Pond, more than two miles

BIRD'S EYE VIEW OF LINCOLN.

in length and about a third of a mile in average breadth, connecting by a short outlet with Comedlasse Pond which empties into Combolass stream and thus makes connection with the middle pond of a chain of three, all of which are drained by a continuation of Combolass stream which crosses the river road and the railroad and empties into the Penobscot, this being the uppermost of the tributaries of that river in Lincoln which contributes four small streams to the Penobscot below the mouth of Combolass stream. The four head streams of Mattakeunk Pond, in Lee, rise in Lincoln and merge into one shortly before crossing the town line.

The population of Lincoln is quite widely distributed but by far the larger part of it is concentrated at Lincoln village, Lincoln centre, and East Lincoln, although there are many residents along the whole ten miles of the river road and also along the road to Topsfield, the Enfield road, and other thoroughfares. The centre of business is at Lincoln village, where there is a railway station, sidetracks communicating with the principal manufacturing establishments so that the trouble and expense of receiving and shipping goods are reduced to a minimum. Lincoln centre has a railway station also, and various mills, shops and stores, besides schools, churches, etc. There is another railway station at South Lincoln, a little more than four miles below Lincoln village. The east part of the town is largely populated, and at East Lincoln is an important post-office, the mail service being quite frequent and the receipts exceeding those of many much more pretentious offices. The town is named in honor of

Governor Lincoln, of Portland, the largest of the original proprietors. Its settlement was begun in 1824, but it was not until the following year that the work of development was entered upon in earnest, and from that date phenomenally rapid progress was made, the early growth of Lincoln being more rapid than that of any other town in Penobscot county. Barely four years elapsed from the time the heavy labor of clearing the ground was begun before the incorporation of the town, the necessary legislative act being passed January 30, 1829, and eleven years later, or in 1840, the town had a population of 1,121. In view of these facts it is hardly necessary to say that the early settlers were intelligent, industrious and enterprising,—qualities which have evidently descended to their successors, for Lincoln is everywhere regarded as one of the most progressive and promising towns in the county. The water power afforded by the Mattanawcook was utilized soon after the settlement of the town, the first mills being located on the site of what is now the lower village. The opening of the military road to Houlton, along the Lincoln side of the Penobscot, was an excellent thing for the town, and the building of the railroad and the subsequent great improvement of its connections have made Lincoln one of the most advantageously located of all the river towns north of Bangor, and in connection with the many natural advantages of the region and the importance which Maine is assuming as a favorable place for the establishment of large manufacturing enterprises justifies the prediction that the future growth of Lincoln will fully bear out the promise of its early years.

Representative Business Men of Lincoln, Me.

MATTANAWCOOK NORMAL ACADEMY,

Lincoln, Me.—As this book is avowedly commercial in character, that is to say, is devoted expressly to the mercantile and manufacturing interests of the region of which it treats, objection may perhaps be made to its containing a notice of the Mattanawcook Normal Academy, as that is so far from being a business institution that its management consider money making of secondary importance, their prime object being to so direct the academy that it shall give as good an education as possible to as many persons as possible. But such an objection would scarcely apply, for the plan of this book calls for mention of all institutions and establishments whose work tends to advance the best interests of the community, and no one will think of denying that the academy has been most helpful to this community and to this section of the State since its incorporation in 1846. Detailed description of the record, resources, aims and prospects of the institution is, of course, quite beyond our power to give in the necessarily limited space available, and we will simply say here is an old established and progressively managed educational institution, utilizing commodious, well-equipped, healthful and beautifully located apartments, capable of accommodating 100 pupils, who will be given every opportunity to gain a thorough training in the English branches, modern languages and music. Conscientious and experienced teachers are provided, the surroundings and the atmosphere are of a character highly favorable to progress, especially when compared with those of large cities or bustling towns, and although it is as true here as elsewhere that "there is no royal road to learning," and each pupil must depend principally upon himself for whatever advancement may be made, still the favorable conditions here present cannot but be of material advantage to every scholar. The residents of Lincoln take great pride in the academy and pupils are assured a hearty reception and kindly treatment, many of the townspeople taking them to board and providing home comforts and home care at almost nominal rates. Mr. Francis H. Fuller is president of the corporation, Oliver H. Chesley vice president ; Mr. Edward T. Fuller is treasurer, and Mr. Meader B. Pinkham is secretary, and any of these gentlemen will furnish further information relative to the academy on application.

MEADER B. PINKHAM, General Merchan-

dise, Lincoln, Me.—A review of the leading business men of Lincoln which contained no mention of Mr. Meader B. Pinkham, would justly be considered as strangely incomplete, for this gentleman is one of the most prominent members of the community, and during his long business career has gained a most enviable reputation for constant attendance to business, and strict integrity. He is a native of this town and has been its treasurer, and on the school committee, also one of the selectmen for fifteen years, and postmaster twelve years. He is engaged in the handling of general merchandise of all kinds, having begun his present enterprise in 1859. The premises made use of are 40×65 feet in dimensions, and contain a well chosen and complete stock, and a large retail business is done. We need hardly say that a merchant having Mr. Pinkham's long experience and ability should be in a position to quote the lowest market rates on dependable goods, and that he does so is well known to our Lincoln readers. Orders are promptly filled, and the high reputation of the enterprise is fully maintained in every respect.

MISSES JORDAN & AVERILL, dealers in

Millinery and Fancy Goods ; orders promptly executed ; reasonable prices ; Lincoln, Me.—We are often told that the highest success in any given line of business is only possible to those who understand it thoroughly in every detail, and a very prominent illustration of this fact is that afforded by the leading position held by the Misses Jordan & Averill among the fashionable milliners of this section, for although these ladies have been located in Lincoln only a few years, they now conduct what is conceded to be one of the representative establishments of the kind in the town. The premises occupied cover an area of some 500 feet, and are fitted up in an attractive manner, while the stock on hand will compare favorably with that carried at any other establishment of the kind in this vicinity. Both these ladies are natives of Lincoln, and their present business was established many years ago by Mrs. Sarah Wilson. The business has been steadily developing from year to year, and it is a noteworthy fact that their patronage is as select as it is extensive. A select stock of the very latest fashionable novelties in millinery and fancy goods is constantly carried, and flowers, velvets and trimmings in general are largely dealt in. Custom millinery work is a very prominent feature of the business and orders are promptly executed at short notice, and at very reasonable prices.

LINCOLN HOUSE, S. H. Clay, Proprietor ; Livery Stable connected ; Free Conch to and from all trains ; Lincoln, Me.—The Lincoln House may properly be called one of the "institutions" of Lincoln, for this hotel has been in existence so many years, and has been so excellently managed from the start that it is well and favorably known to all whom business or pleasure call frequently to the town. The present proprietor, Mr. S. H. Clay, assumed sole control in 1889, he having previously been associated with Mr. C. M. Woods in the proprietorship of this hotel for about one year. Mr. Clay is a native of Springfield, Me., and is a well known and highly esteemed hotel keeper. The Lincoln House has fifty guest rooms, and is conveniently and very pleasantly located. It is a thoroughly neat and well kept hotel in every respect, and the most fastidious can find no reasonable fault with either the house or its appointments, the beds and other furnishings being modern and comfortable in style, while the service is remarkably efficient, being prompt, intelligent and obliging. The *cuisine* will be found very satisfactory, the table being supplied with an abundance of seasonable food at all times of the year, and is neatly served. There is a good stable connected with the house at which teams of all kinds may be obtained at moderate rates, and at very short notice, while free coaches are on hand to meet all trains. As Lincoln is in the immediate vicinity of hunting and fishing territory, sportsmen and tourists will find this hotel just the place to make a halt for a few days' comfort and rest, and where they can get points about hunting and fishing to the best advantage.

F. H. TUPPER, Druggist, Lincoln, Me.— People are very apt to wonder how the proprietor of a "General store" can keep track of all the articles he handles, and are not slow to excuse the frequent mistakes made in such establishments, on the grounds that errors are unavoidable under such circumstances. And yet we question if the average general store contains such a large variety of articles as may be found in a first class modern pharmacy. Such a one for instance as is conducted by Mr. F. H. Tupper in this town. The extreme scarcity of errors in a well equipped drug store speaks volumes for the ability and care of those having such establishments in charge, but the public accept this condition of affairs as a matter of course and give but little credit to those to whom credit is due. Mr. Tupper has qualified himself for his profession by years of practical labor in a drug store, and legally by receiving from the State Board of Pharmacy a certificate of registration dated May 14, 1885. He carries a large and varied stock, including a complete assortment of drugs, medicines, and chemicals of every description. He has recently completed his formula, and placed upon the market a medicine which ought to find its way into every home. People who have used his "Compound Sarsaparilla" offer valuable testimony. It is not a patent medicine, as he has posted conspicuously the formula, and everyone can subject it to their family physician and he must admit that all the ingredients act directly on the four great organs (the producers of health or disease) viz., the *stomach*, *liver*, kidneys and blood. Remember he does not doctor the *list* of symptoms and effects but only doctors the four great organs which produce health or disease and when they perform their natural functions, the long list of symptoms and effects will disappear; it is a constitutional treatment with nature's remedies, roots, herbs and barks, try it. You cannot lose your money, for you are sure to receive a benefit. Special attention is given to prescription trade and no pains is spared to fill all orders in an accurate

manner, and at very reasonable prices. The store is 20×50 feet in dimensions, recently fitted, and contains a fine stock of toilet and fancy articles, druggists sundries, etc. Mr. Tupper has recently taken the agency for the celebrated "Estey organs" and pianos, which he sells cheap for cash, or on installments on easy terms, any make desired furnished at very lowest prices. He is a lover of fine horses and can most always show a few good ones. A former resident of Bangor and a native of Harrington, Me., and succeeded to the business of A. D. Wilson, established over fifteen years ago.

E. A. WEATHERBEE, dealer in Hardware, Stoves and Tinware, Guns, Ammunition, Paints, Oils, etc. Lincoln, Me.—Of late years there have been great improvements in certain lines of manufacture, and in no industry has much greater progress been made than in that relating to the production of stoves and ranges. Some of the parlor stoves now on the market combine beauty and efficiency to a remarkable degree, but there are others which are of but little use except for purely ornamental purposes, for their designers in attaining beauty of form and decoration seriously injured the heating qualities. However, there is no use of purchasing a stove defective in any respect, and the best way to avoid doing so is to buy of a dealer such as Mr. E. A. Weatherbee, for he has had sufficient experience to he thoroughly familiar with the leading styles of heating and cooking stoves, and he handles none which he has reason to believe will not give satisfaction. This undertaking was founded a great many years ago, by Mr. A. W. Weatherbee, and after changing owners several times, came under the management of the present proprietor in 1889, who is a native of Springfield, Me., and very well known in this town, having been supervisor of schools. The premises utilized by him comprises a store, 40×40 feet in dimensions and a large stock of hardware, stoves and tinware, besides guns, ammunition, paints, oils, etc., is constantly carried. The lowest market rates are quoted, and all kinds of repairs for stoves, ranges, etc., are done in the most workman-like manner at short notice.

MRS. E. C. CLARK, Millinery, Fancy Goods, Dry Goods and Notions, Lincoln, Me.—It is inevitable that in every community there should be establishments which either on account of their long standing, the excellence of the service provided, or both, should be universally considered to be the leaders in their particular line, and among such it is fitting that prominent mention should be made of that conducted by Mrs. E. C. Clark, in this town. This business has been carried on by Mrs. Clark for ten years. She is a native of Hamden, Me., and has a large circle of friends throughout this vicinity. Her long and varied experience is of course of great advantage to her in the filling of orders for the millinery work, and as her taste is unexceptionally correct, it is not surprising that no difficulty should be met with in satisfying the most fastidious customers. The store is about 800 feet in dimensions, and contains a beautiful stock of millinery and fancy goods, and notions, comprising the latest fashionable novelties, for Mrs. Clark makes it a rule to give her patrons the earliest chance to select from the newest styles. Uniformly moderate rates are quoted.

DR. C. P. SMALL,

DENTIST

LINCOLN, - - MAINE.

Having had fifteen years practice in dentistry, five years of which was spent with Dr. Philander Evans, of Bangor, and also having had the benefit of the Boston Dental School during the years of 1880 and 1881, I am prepared to perform all the branches of dentistry in a scientific and satisfactory manner. My office is equipped with the most modern appliances, and everything arranged for the comfort of patients. A specialty is made of gold and porcelain crowns, being set on natural roots. I also make a specialty of administering Mayo's vegetable and nitrous oxide gas. I have one of the best obtunders used in the profession for the painless extraction of teeth.

People from out of town should make appointments by mail, as the last two weeks in each month I shall visit the towns of Kingman, Mattawamkeag, Medway, Winn, Lee and Springfield.

HARRISON PIPER, Watches, Clocks and Jewelry, Silverware, etc.; Fine Watch Repairing a specialty ; Orders by mail will receive prompt attention ; Lincoln, Me.—Perhaps there are few among the business men or residents of this town who realize that this is one of the oldest established houses conducting business without change in the name or interruption to business in the town. That such is the fact is claimed by the proprietor, Mr. Harrison Piper, he having established his business here thirty-two years ago, and as the residents of Lincoln have a well deserved reputation for patronizing home establishments, the wisdom of this course is well indicated by the general high standing of the local retail business enterprises. There is little encouragement for a dealer to endeavor to offer unusual inducements, when he knows that all having important purchases to make will visit some adjoining town, but when the contrary is the case, the result is soon perceptible. Take the store conducted by Mr. Piper for example, and the truth of the principles we have hinted at will be made manifest. Mr. Piper carries as fine a stock of watches, clocks and jewelry, silver ware, etc., as can be found in this section, and his prices cannot be discounted by any retailer of whom we have any knowledge. Mr. Piper is a practical watchmaker, and makes a specialty of fine watch repairing. He is a native of Great Falls, N. H., has held the position of town treasurer, and been a selectman, and is now postmaster, so that he is well and favorably known throughout this vicinity.

PORTER & MILLS, dealers in Burial Caskets and Robes ; at the store of C. W. Porter, Lincoln, Me.—The enterprise conducted by Messrs. Porter & Mills in the store of C. W. Porter in this town, is most certainly deserving of prominent mention among the leading and typical undertakings of this section, for it was inaugurated about four years ago, and has held a leading position ever since. The present firm is composed of C. W. Porter, who is a native of Searsport, and P. J. Mills, who is a native of Lincoln. They deal in burial caskets and robes, etc., etc., while all the newest and best improved methods have been added to the equipment of the establishment, and the finest undertaking work is executed. Employment is given to only competent assistants, and as for the facilities at hand, it is only necessary to say that they are amply sufficient to fully maintain the established reputation of this concern for promptness and thoroughness. This firm have the agency in this section for J. Newman & Son's floral designs, flowers and emblems of all descriptions, furnished at short notice, as direct communication by telegraph is had with the above named house, the Commercial Union Telegraph office being located here.

G. STETSON, dealer in Fruit, Confectionery, Nuts, Cigars, Tobacco and Fancy Groceries, Clothing, Hats, Caps and Robes, Lincoln, Me.—Such a stock as is carried by Mr. G. Stetson, cannot be adequately described in the limited space at our command, for it is so varied and so complete in every department that to merely name the commodities it comprises would more than exhaust our space as well as the patience of our readers. But as a matter of fact such a procedure is quite unnecessary, for the Lincoln public thoroughly understand that patrons of this store are given an exceptionally large and desirable assortment to choose from, and they know that not only staple goods, but also the latest novelties are well represented. It would be surprising were not Mr. Stetson well appreciated by this time, for he has been identified with his present enterprise for nearly a half a century, having begun operations in 1846. Mr. Stetson is a native of Eastport, Me., and the premises used cover an area of some 800 feet in dimensions, and among the more prominent commodities kept in stock may be mentioned fruit, nuts, confectionery, cigars, tobacco, and fancy groceries, clothing, hats, caps and robes, etc., etc. A large family trade is enjoyed as the goods are chosen expressly for family use, and are thoroughly reliable in quality and low in price. Efficient assistants are employed, so that prompt and polite attention is assured all callers.

S. L. KIMBALL, dealer in Meats, Groceries, Provisions, and such other Goods as are Usually Found in a First class Store, Lincoln, Me.—Among the many general merchandise stores to be found in Lincoln and vicinity, that conducted by Mr. S. L. Kimball is deserving of prominent and favorable mention, not so much on account of any single exceptional inducement which its proprietor offers to the public, as by reason of the "all round" character of the advantages extended, or in other words Mr. Kimball does not make a "leader" of any one line of goods, selling them below cost and more than making up on other articles, but he does quote the lowest market rates on all the commodities he handles, and he spares no pains to furnish goods that will give the best of satisfaction. This gentleman began operations in 1880, he is a native of this State and the store occupied covers an area of some 700 feet, being sufficiently spacious to accommodate a large stock of meats, groceries and provisions, besides clothing, boots and shoes, crockery and glassware, also such other goods as are usually found in a first class general store. Cigars and tobacco are also kept in stock Orders are promptly and accurately filled and every article is sold under a guarantee that it will prove precisely as represented.

MAIN STREET, LOOKING EAST.

HISTORICAL SKETCH OF WINN, ME.

Winn lies on the east bank of the Penobscot River and is in the eastern quarter of Penobscot county and very near to the Aroostook county line, being separated from the latter by a single township, that of Mattawamkeag, which bounds Winn on the north. It is bounded on the east by Webster Plantation, on the south by Lee, on the southwest by Lincoln and on the northwest by the Penobscot River, the frontage of the town on that stream amounting to about five miles. Opposite Winn, in the Penobscot, are the "Five Islands" after which the town was at one time named, and there are also several other islands near at hand the principal ones being Brown, Snow and Gordon islands. Winn is at the head of steamboat navigation on the Penobscot and its early history is closely identified with that of steamboating on that noble stream.

The township is quite regular in outline, with the exception of the side turned towards the river, has an average length of about five and one-half miles, an average breadth of about five miles, and an area of 22,040 acres. The principal stream is the Mattakeunk, which is the result of the union of two water-courses known as the East and the West Branches. The West Branch enters from Lee about two miles from Winn's southeast corner, flows through the village of East Winn, where it affords a valuable water power, and about four miles farther along unites with the East branch, which enters from Springfield at the southeast corner of Winn and flows four and a half miles through the town before it reaches the point of junction. The resulting stream — the Mattakeunk — is quite broad but is very short, it being only a few miles long, as it takes a direct northerly course and empties into the Mattawamkeag River within the town of Winn. The latter stream enters near the northeast corner of the town, describes a small semi-circle and regains the north town line and then dips down again, this time making a much longer curve, recrossing the northern boundary and flowing through Mattawamkeag a few miles to the Penobscot. There is a water power at Gordon Falls in the Mattawamkeag River within Winn's limits and there are several powers on Mattakeunk stream. There are various other streams in town but they are not of sufficient importance to merit description.

Manufacturing is carried on to a considerable extent, the production of sole leather being by far the most important local industry, as a very large tannery is located here. Long and short lumber are also manufactured, as are boots and shoes, harness, carriage and smith work, etc. There are some excellent stores at Winn village which is the trade centre of a very considerable extent of country. It is located on the Maine Central Railroad and contains two handsome churches, a very large hotel and other public buildings, besides the immense tannery previously referred to and a number of attractive private residences.

Winn was incorporated in 1857 but was settled many years before that date, the first settler, Joseph Snow, making his appearance early in the spring of 1820. As there were no special inducements offered by this region the work of settlement went on very slowly and what few settlers there were were scattered about, the present village of Winn not being established until steamboat navigation on the Penobscot had become an accomplished fact, when the steamboat landing at " Five Islands " became the nucleus around which gathered stores, shops and dwellings.

The first boat reached this point in the latter part of 1847, and from that date to 1863, when the tannery was established, the growth of the village was dependent almost entirely upon the steamboat service. The European and North American Railway reached Winn in the fall of 1869, and has aided the development of the town although not so largely as had been expected.

About 1852 the inhabitants of River Township No. 4, or "Snowville" as it was also called, in honor of the first settler, were organized as Five Islands Plantation, and April 8, 1857, the town of Winn was duly incorporated. It was named in honor of John M. Winn, who at the time of incorporation was the principal proprietor of the township, but not long afterward became financially embarrassed and finally lost every dollar he had in the world.

Winn is growing steadily in both population and wealth and its growth is of that healthy, substantial character which inspires confidence and ensures permanency. There are some fine farms in town, the local industries are flourishing and the local trade interests are prospering, so that Winn has fairly entered upon the last decade of the present century under favorable auspices and may reasonably be expected to make pronounced progress during its remaining years.

—

Representative Business Men of Winn, Me.

HENRY POOR & SON, Tanners of Hemlock Sole Leather; C. P. Van Vleck, Agent, Winn, Me.—The magnitude of the tanning industry in Maine is not appreciated outside the sections where it is most extensively carried on, and many would never think of including leather among the most important products of the State, and yet it is entitled to that distinction, not only by reason of the quantity, but also the quality of the product, Maine sole leather of the higher grade being unsurpassed in the market. The house of Henry Poor & Son, having its main office at No. 60 South street, Boston, Mass., is known to the trade as one of the largest producers of hemlock sole leather, and it is a significant fact that the business conducted by this firm has steadily and rapidly increased since its inception some sixty years ago. The tanneries now utilized include one at Winn, built in 1864 ; one at Medway, built in 1870 ; one at Lowell, purchased in 1881 ; and one at Lincoln, purchased in 1883. They are fitted up with improved machinery, which is run by steam, with the exception of the Lowell tannery, which is driven by water power. Employment is given to 165 men inside, and in bark peeling season about 600 men are employed, also in winter about 200 teams, and the total capacity of the four tanneries is about 2,000 tons per year. Mr. C. P. Van Vleck is agent for all of them, he having his headquarters at Winn, where the concern maintains a heavily stocked supply store. Messrs. Henry Poor & Son furnish sole leather to many of the most prominent boot and shoe manufacturers in the country, and their product is accepted as the standard wherever introduced, and finds a ready market notwithstanding the large amount turned out.

KATAHDIN HOUSE, Winn, Me.; Mattawamkeag House, Mattawamkeag, Me. ; First-class Livery Stable connected with both houses ; S. B. Gates, Proprietor, Winn, Me.—Many strangers visit this section on business, and many more on pleasure trips, so that there is very considerable demand for hotel accommodations, and we are happy to say that that demand is very satisfactorily supplied by the Katahdin House at Winn, and the Mattawamkeag House at Mattawamkeag, Mr. S. B. Gates of Winn being proprietor of both hotels. He is a native of Lincoln, Me., and is very generally and favorably known among the travelling public as well as among the residents of this portion of the State, for he has carried on the Katahdin House since 1875, and the Mattawamkeag House since 1884, and as he has always done his best to make his guests feel at home, it is natural that he should have made many friends among them and gained an enviable reputation as " a square man who knows how to keep a hotel," as one of the most enthusiastic sportsmen who visit this section describes Mr. Gates. Employment is given to eight assistants at Winn, and to nine at Mattawamkeag, and each hotel can very comfortably accommodate fifty guests, but double that number have been accommodated during "a rush," for this region is very largely visited at certain seasons. There is a first-class livery stable connected with each house, and excellent teams may be obtained at short notice and at moderate rates. Mr. Gates carefully supervises both houses, sees that the service is maintained at a high standard of efficiency, promotes the comfort of his guests in all possible ways, and in short, carries out the policy which has made the two hotels under his charge rank with the most popular in Maine.

C. J. CARLL, Undertaker and dealer in Caskets ; also Harness Made and Repaired ; Winn, Me.—Mr. C. J. Carll is a native of Belfast, Me , but during the twenty-five years that he has carried on business in Winn has become so thoroughly identified with the interests of the town as to be looked upon as a representative citizen in the full sense of the word. Mr. Carll has had long and varied business experience as an undertaker, and is prepared to fill all orders entrusted to him in that capacity with fidelity, intelligence and dispatch. He will assume charge of funerals, and furnish everything that is required, his facilities enabling him to execute all commissions at very short notice, and at uniformly moderate rates. He deals extensively in agricultural implements and all kinds of seeds, and furniture, etc., and is also a maker and repairer of harness. The premises occupied cover about 1,000 square feet, together with a storeroom. The assortment of goods is sufficiently extensive and complete to enable all purses and all tastes to be suited, and those who wish to obtain articles that will prove precisely as represented, at the lowest market rates would do well to give Mr. Carll a call.

WINN DRUG STORE.

H. H. DeBECK, M.D., Manager,

WINN, MAINE.

One generally feels considerable hesitation in giving advice as to what physician shall be consulted or at what pharmacy prescriptions shall be compounded, for the consequences of advising wrongly in either case are too grave to be lightly assumed. Still, we feel perfectly sure that all who may patronize the establishment conducted by H. H. De Beck, M. D., manager of the " Winn Drug Store," will have no reason to regret having done so, for we know that the stock of drugs, medicines and chemicals there carried is full and complete; also a full line of surgical appliances is carried in stock. Dr. De Beck may be depended upon to compound every prescription with which he is entrusted with care. He opened his present store in 1886, which is well arranged and fitted up for the purposes for which it is used. Dr. De Beck endeavors to keep only pure and fresh drugs, etc., and secures that end as far as possible by procuring his supplies from the most reputable sources. He is very moderate in his charges, and employs one efficient assistant, thus being able to fill all orders without undue delay.

H. H. BLACKWELL, Jeweler and Watch Repairer, Winn, Me.—Mr. H. H. Blackwell is a jeweler, dealer in, and repairer of watches, having begun operations here in 1867. In 1873 he went West, and returned in 1890. Mr. Blackwell is a native of Norridgewock, Me. It is unfortunate that with the great increase in the number of fine watches in general use of late years, there has not been a corresponding increase in the number of those capable of repairing the same, for as mat-

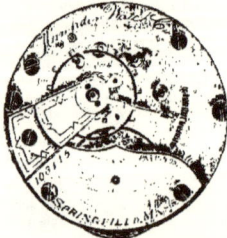

ters now are the better the watch is, the more liable its owner is to experience difficulty in having it repaired properly. That this is a correct statement of the case, no one acquainted with the facts will dispute, and therefore we feel that in directing our readers to an establishment where a specialty is made of repairing watches, we are giving them information which may save them time, money and trouble. Mr. H. H. Blackwell carries a good assortment of watches and jewelry, which it will please him to show, and will pay for the time spent in examination. He gives personal attention to the repairing of watches and jewelry in all its branches and his prices are moderate.

MRS. J. A. BRADMAN, Millinery, Fancy Goods, Dry Goods, Boots and Shoes, Ladies Furnishings, Winn.—The business conducted by Mrs. J. A. Bradman had its inception in 1884 in Mattawamkeag, and was carried on there till 1889, when it was started in this town. The premises are fitted up for the tasteful display of her large stock which consists of a complete line of millinery and fancy goods, dry goods, boots and shoes, and ladies furnishings, etc., etc. Mrs. Bradman has a large order trade and it is with pleasure that we recommend her goods and establishment to the favorable attention of all our readers who have not patronized her; here they can obtain fresh goods of the latest designs and newest styles at fair and reasonable prices. Dressmaking is also done in connection with the other business. Mrs. Bradman only employs competent assistants, and keeps on hand a well assorted and carefully selected stock of everything usually to be found in a first class establishment of this kind, and her facilities for obtaining goods at first hands and at the lowest possible figures are well known and recognized and her experience leads her to anticipate and meet the wants of the public, in a prompt and satisfactory manner, judging from her large number of patrons. Mr. J. A. Bradman is prepared to do carriage and sign painting in the best manner and at very reasonable rates.

J. E. & F. C. ESTES, dealers in Mowing Machines, Sewing Machines, Horse Rakes, Wagons, Sleighs, Hides, Pelts, Furs, etc. Also Groceries, Meat and Short Lumber, Winn, Me.—The enterprise conducted by Messrs. J. E. & F. C. Estes is deserving of particularly prominent mention in any review of the representative business undertakings of Winn and vicinity, not only on account of the great extent to which it has been developed, but also by reason of the high personal standing its proprietors have in the community, and the fact that they are among the oldest established merchants in town, having begun operations in 1875. Messrs. J. E. & F. C. Estes, are both natives of Vasselboro, Me. The premises occupied by the firm in this town comprise a store 22×80 feet in dimensions, also a basement 22×60 feet, together with a store house, so that there is abundant room to accommodate a large stock, and this room is fully used, the assortment on hand being remarkably varied and complete in every department. It is made up of mowing machines, sewing machines, horse rakes, wagons, sleighs, hides, pelts, furs, etc., etc., together with a stock of fine groceries, meats and short lumber, etc., which latter have been added to their old business about one year since. These articles are in every instance guaranteed to prove precisely as represented and are offered at prices that will bear the most severe examination and comparison, for this firm have always made it a rule not to allow themselves to be undersold in the handling of dependable goods.

GUY W. MERRILL,

PHOTOGRAPHER

WINN, MAINE.

J. E. ESTES, Attorney at Law, Winn, Me.— It is perfectly safe to make the assertion that no one in this section of the State is more prominent in law matters than Mr. J. E. Estes, for this gentleman has been identified with such interests, for many years, in Winn, and as no mercantile enterprises can be successfully carried on nowadays without competent legal advice at times, for questions are continually arising which require extensive knowledge of the law and of precedents in order to answer them satisfactorily, and the demands of modern business are so exacting that it is simply impossible for any man however able to properly attend to them and at the same time to keep himself free from legal complications without that assistance which only an experienced attorney at law can render. The great majority of business men appreciate this fact and the extensive legal practice enjoyed by Mr. J. E. Estes, is the natural consequence of this appreciation, and of the general knowledge of his long and varied experience in the profession, having had exceptional opportunities to become familiar with the court's practice.

A. J. LEE, Dry Goods, Groceries and Jewelry, Winn, Me.—Among those establishments which merit mention in this book, that conducted by Mr. A. J. Lee, should be given a place, for although this store makes no great pretensions still it is worthy of the most liberal patronage for the simple reason that no goods are sold under false pretences, every article being guaranteed to prove just as represented in every respect. This business was founded a great many years ago by Messrs. Lovejoy & Hall, who were succeeded by T. R. Joy & Co., they carrying it on for some fifteen years, and up to 1891, when the present proprietor took its management. The premises used consist of one store 25×65 feet in dimensions, and a large retail trade is done in dry goods of all kinds, groceries and jewelry, etc. Mr. Lee who is a native of Sebec, Me., does not claim to sell lower than everybody else or to be constantly offering goods "below cost," but he is content with a small margin of profit, and a dollar will go about as far in this store as at any similar establishment in town. Orders are promptly filled, every caller receiving careful and polite attention. The post-office is in this store.

HENRY JARVIS, dealer in Groceries, Dry Goods, Boots, Shoes and Rubbers, Hats, Caps, Clothing, etc., also Fresh and Salt Meats and Fish, Winn, Me.—Of course in the compilation of a book of this kind it is not always easy to determine the proper degree of prominence to give the various business enterprises of which mention is made, but this difficulty is not present in all classes by any means as there are certain undertakings the representative character of which is so apparent as to be obvious, making their title to a leading position in any review of the section's business houses clear beyond dispute. In this class must be placed the establishment carried on by Henry Jarvis, in this town. For the many years that this undertaking has been conducted, and the unsurpassed reputation for fair dealing and enterprise enjoyed by the manager combine to make it representative in the full sense of the word. The enterprise in question was founded many years ago, by Mr. G. H. Haynes, and so continued till 1884, when the present proprietor assumed its management. The premises occupied comprise one store 40×100 feet in size, and the stock on hand is large enough to test its capacity for it is exceptionally complete and comprises groceries, dry goods, boots, shoes and rubbers, hats, caps, clothing, etc., etc. Also fresh and salt meats and fish, etc. Employment is given to efficient assistants and customers are promptly served while the character of the trade is enough to prove that the proprietor handles only reliable goods and quotes low prices.

BIRD'S EYE VIEW OF MATTAWAMKEAG.

HISTORICAL SKETCH OF MATTAWAMKEAG.

Mattawamkeag is the most northerly of the Penobscot county towns along the east bank of the Penobscot river, it being bounded on the north by Molunkus and Macwahoc plantations in Aroostook county. Kingman bounds it on the east; Webster plantation and Winn on the south, and Woodville plantation or Indian township on the west, it being separated from the latter by the Penobscot river. It is fifty-eight miles north-northeast of Bangor on the Maine Central railroad at its point of junction with the Canadian Pacific railroad, and the former road has extensive repair shops, etc., at Mattawamkeag village, making it the most important place on its line, Bangor, of course, excepted. The extreme breadth of the township is six and one-half miles and it is a little more than five miles across its narrowest part, while its eastern line is nearly five and one-half miles long and its western boundary line or river frontage is five and two-thirds miles in length, the area of the tract being slightly less than that of an evenly surveyed township.

There are no important lakes or ponds and the largest and most useful stream is the Mattawamkeag River, from which the town is named. The name of the stream is obviously of Indian origin and is said to mean "a river with many rocks at its mouth." The river rises in Aroostook county and after passing through Drew plantation and Kingman enters Mattawamkeag a mile and a quarter above the southeast corner of the township, dips twice below the border of Winn on the south and then takes a straight northwest course to the Penobscot into which it empties at Mattawamkeag village, its channel from its first point of entrance into the town being about seven miles in length, and the character of the stream being very favorable for the operations of the lumbermen, as is also that of the Mattaseunk stream which enters the town from Molunkus and flows across its northwest corner to the Penobscot. Both the Mattawamkeag and the Mattaseunk receive various tributaries during their passage through the town and are valuable streams whose facilities are largely availed of. Mills were built as early as 1805 by Alexander Gordon at what are now known as Gordon's Falls, in the Mattawamkeag, but they were burned by the Indians in 1812.

Mattawamkeag was formerly known as Township No. 1, East Indian Purchase, and the first settlement was made very early in the century as is indicated by the building of the mills in 1805, but it was not until 1854 that it was organized as a plantation, and it did not become an incorporated town until February, 1860. But since that date its growth has been continuous and pronounced, and at times exceptionally rapid, the tendency of late years being to out-do all previous records. From 1860 to 1870 the population increased from 260 to 356; from 1870 to 1880 it grew to 456; and in 1890 it had amounted to 633; the valuation of estates at that time amounting to $139,642, as compared with an estate valuation of $77,768 in 1880. The first train reached Mattawamkeag in November, 1869, and this is an important date in the history of the town as it owes the greater part of its prosperity to the excellence of its railway facilities, although the possession of these is due, of course, to the natural advantages enjoyed by the town.

The enterprise and ability of some of the early settlers must also be considered in summing up the reasons for Mattawamkeag's development, and prominent among these men is Captain Samuel W. Coombs, who was the fourth permanent settler, he coming in 1835, and for a period of forty-seven years being actively engaged in the surveying of land and lumber. Captain Coombs has done much to advance the best interests of the town, has held various public offices, and is one of the most widely known and highly respected residents of Penobscot county, and an acknowledged authority on matters relating to Mattawamkeag's history.

The manufactures of the town include the production of long and short lumber, smith work, and picture frames, besides the important industries carried on at the M. C. R. R. locomotive works and at the M. C. R. R. car shops. There are about half a dozen general stores besides other mercantile establishments and a couple of hotels; Mattawamkeag village being the centre of trade for miles around as well as an important railway and stage station, and being the terminus of stage lines to Medway and Patten. The mail, express and telegraphic services are excellent, and, in short, Mattawamkeag possesses all the conveniences and facilities of an enterprising and prosperous modern town, including good schools, adequate religious facilities, and prosperous fraternal organizations, the latter including Masonic associations and a grange of Patrons of Husbandry.

Representative Business Men of Mattawamkeag.

F. A. JAMES & CO., dealers in Groceries, Meats, etc.; also Proprietors of Livery Stable, Mattawamkeag. Me.—Many a housekeeper is looking for just such an establishment as that carried on by Messrs. F. A. James & Co., located in this town, and we take pleasure in commending this enterprise to such inquirers, for we know that Messrs. James & Co.'s methods are such to please and we know that those who have business dealings with this concern are outspoken in their approval of the accommodations offered Operations were begun in 1888, and the trade has since steadily increased. The firm consists of F. A. James and A. W. Scott, both natives of this State. The store occupied is 20×30 feet in size, and the stock on hand is large and varied, which includes groceries of all kinds, and meats, etc. It will be seen that the greater part of the household food supply may be obtained of Messrs. James & Co., and as their prices are all that can be reasonably desired as regards fairness, etc., it is well worth while giving them a call. The groceries and provisions comprise the best the markets afford, and the canned goods handled are varied in kind and best in quality, while everything handled in stock is received direct from the producers and are quoted at prices as low as the lowest. Four competent assistants are employed and all customers are served in a polite and intelligent manner. This firm are proprietors of a livery stable where good teams may be had at reasonable rates. Adjoining the store of this firm is the fancy goods and millinery department of Mrs. A. W. Scott.

W. H. LIBBEY, dealer in Dry Goods, Groceries of all kinds, Boots, Shoes, etc., Mattawamkeag, Me.—Other things being equal, it is of course advisable to procure as large a proportion of whatever goods may be required as possible at one store, for time and trouble are saved by so doing, and few of us have any time to throw away. It is sometimes argued that those who make a specialty of certain goods can offer greater inducements than general dealers, but "the proof of the pudding is in the eating," and those who have made practical comparison of the advantages offered by Mr. W. H. Libbey, with those held out by special dealers, are convinced that he does as well by his customers as any retailer can do. This business was established many years ago, and about ten years since passed under the control of the present proprietor who is a native of Maine and who has increased the business so much that three assistants are required to give the many orders prompt and careful attention. The premises occupied are spacious and are 20×40 feet in dimensions, together with a storeroom, and contains an extensive and varied stock of dry goods, groceries of all kinds, boots, shoes, etc., and other commodities too numerous to make detailed mention of, a catalogue of it would exhaust many times our available space, but the residents of Mattawamkeag know that Mr. Libbey constantly carries a full assortment, and that the goods may be safely depended upon to prove as represented.

G. F. STRATTON & CO., Meat, Fish and Groceries, Mattawamkeag, Me.—It is by catering especially to the family trade that Messrs. Stratton & Smith have worked up the liberal patronage they now enjoy in the sale of meat, fish and groceries, in this town, and none who have observed the methods by which this establishment has been advanced to its present popularity can begrudge them the success attained, for it has been won not by belittling competitors and seeking to injure any man, but by conscientious, intelligent and untiring work of the hardest kind, Mr. G. F. Stratton is a native of Presque Isle, Me., and Mr. C. A. Smith of Mattawamkeag. They founded their present business in Mattawamkeag, in 1891. Spacious premises are occupied and employment is given to only competent assistants, which enables them to fill all orders with promptness and accuracy. The stock on hand is a full and varied one, ranging from tea to flour, and from molasses to kerosene oil, besides a choice assortment of meats and fish of all kinds is carried, meats and fish forming an important part of the business. Fresh fish is received from the market every Friday morning. The prices are reasonable and customers of this house can depend on getting a fair equivalent for their money. This firm have reason to take special pride in the goods furnished to patrons, for it is impossible to find their superior elsewhere.

GEO. W. SMITH, dealer in Dry Goods, Groceries, Corn, Flour and Provisions, Hardware, Cutlery, Paints, Oils, Crockery and Glass-Ware, Patent Medicines, Fancy Goods, Stationery, etc., Mattawamkeag, Me.—This enterprise was founded by Mr. Asa Smith in 1835, and carried on by him for many years, the present proprietor, Mr. Geo. W. Smith, assuming control in 1862. He is a native of Haynesville, Me. Mr. Smith deals very extensively in general merchandise, the store occupied being 40×50 feet in size, the stock being as large as it is varied and we have only to say that among the more important of the commodities, it includes, are full lines of dry goods, groceries, corn, flour and provisions, hardware, cutlery, paints, oils, glass-ware and crockery, patent medicines, fancy goods, and stationery, etc. The quality is as noteworthy as the quantity, for although Mr. Smith handles all the standard grades of goods, he deals in no goods he cannot guarantee will prove as represented. Bottom prices are quoted in every department of the business, while country produce is taken at the highest market prices in exchange for goods. Polite and competent assistants are employed and orders are filled with promptness. Mr. Smith is a selectman, postmaster and American Express Company's agent.

INTERNATIONAL HOUSE, W. R. Stratton, Proprietor, Mattawamkeag, Me.—It is by no means an agreeable task to recommend a hotel to a man unless you know what his tastes are, for some individuals go in for "style" alone and will put up with comfortless accommodations and poor service as long as they know they are in a "high toned" house, while others put comfort before style and don't care how exclusive and aristocratic a house is as long as it is homelike and respectable. But in recommending the International House to our readers we will avoid all possible misunderstanding by saying at the outset that this hotel is run on the assumption that the public want pleasant rooms, comfortable beds, an abundance of good substantial food and prompt and polite attendance, and that they don't want to pay fancy prices, but are willing to pay a fair amount for homelike accommodations. The present proprietor, Mr. W. R. Stratton assumed control in 1887, he is a native of Maine and does all in his power to secure the comfort of guests and is very popular among the patrons of the house, who speak in the highest terms of his readiness to furnish any desired information and to make things as easy and pleasant as possible for strangers in town. The house can accommodate some fifty guests, and the table is bountifully supplied at all seasons of the year, while the cooking and service are excellent, and the prices are moderate. This house is pleasantly located, is about 100 yards from railroad station and is very convenient. Anyone wishing for a quiet and pleasant place to pass the summer, will find this a good place to tarry and where the boarding rates are very moderate.

F. A. GREENWOOD, Dry Goods, Boots and Shoes, Meat and Fish, Mattawamkeag, Me.—The establishment carried on by Mr. F. A. Greenwood, is as fine an example of a first-class country store as can be found in Maine, and is worthy of much more extended mention than the limitations of space will enable us to give it, for the stock carried is so varied and the business has so many important departments that a full description of the enterprise would occupy a good deal of room. It was inaugurated some five years ago by the present proprietor, who is a native of Canada, and is one of the best-known business men in this section, being highly esteemed for his active and progressive but strictly honorable methods. The premises made use of consist of a store, covering some 600 square feet and a meat room, and among the more important commodities included in the stock may be mentioned dry goods, boots, shoes, meat and fish. No fancy prices are quoted in any department and indeed Mr. Greenwood makes a practice of furnishing all the articles which he deals in, at the lowest market rates, orders will be promptly and accurately filled under his personal supervision. In addition to the above business, Mr. Greenwood carries a full supply of coffins and caskets, together with a complete assortment of funeral goods. Embalming is also done.

MRS. C. A. HAYNES, Dry and Fancy Goods, Millinery, Mattawamkeag, Me.—The value and desirability of a stock of goods depend more upon quality than quantity, and this is particularly the case where such articles as millinery and fancy goods are concerned, so it may be safely asserted that no more attractive assortment can be found in Mattawamkeag than that offered by Mrs. C. A. Haynes, for this is selected with exceptional skill and care, and comprises the latest fashionable novelties, while it is sufficiently varied to suit all tastes and all purses. Mrs. Haynes began operations some years ago and has built up a very desirable trade, her success being due not only to the attractiveness of the goods offered, but also to the moderate charges made in every department of the business and the promptness with which orders are filled. Millinery, dry and fancy goods, and notions of all kinds, etc., may be obtained here at the lowest market rates, together with choice fancy goods in great variety. Custom work is given prompt and painstaking attention and the results attained will surely prove satisfactory to the most critical. Callers are always welcome, goods being cheerfully shown and prices quoted. Mrs. Haynes has a few desirable house lots situated on one of the pleasantest streets in Mattawamkeag, which she would like to sell.

BIRD'S EYE VIEW OF KINGMAN.

HISTORICAL SKETCH OF KINGMAN, ME.

Kingman is a comparatively new town in a quite recently settled region, it lying near the border of the great Aroostook wilderness and the first settlement in the tract, being made less than thirty years ago, although it was organized as a plantation in 1859. The north and east part, including about 900 of the 15,000 acres included in the present township, belonged to the Waterson and Pray purchase and the remainder was granted by Massachusetts to Camden to aid that town to bridge Duck Trap Stream. The tract was originally known as Township No. 6, range 4, north of Bingham's purchase, and was organized as McCrillis Plantation, July 4, 1859. At that time it was entirely wild land covered by a dense forest, the first recorded settlement not being made until 1864. March 28, 1866, it was re-organized as Independence Plantation and so remained until February, 1873, when it was incorporated as a town and named in honor of R. S. Kingman, of the firm of Shaw & Kingman who established the great tannery which has done and is doing so much to develop the town. Some idea of the magnitude and rapidity of this development may be gained from the fact that from 1870 to 1880 (during which decade the tannery was established) the population of the plantation increased from 183 to 546 ; the number of polls from 16 to 165, and the valuation of estates from $30,677.00 to $75,-455.00. The 1890 census gives the town a population of 671 and an estate valuation of $126,154.00. Kingman is located in the east part of Penobscot county, 66 miles north-northeast of Bangor, on the Maine Central Railroad. It is bounded on the north by Macwahoc, in Aroostook county, on the east by Drew, on the south by Webster Plantation and on the west by Mattawamkeag. The township is considerably smaller than the average, for although it is of standard length — six miles — it is not quite four miles in breadth, its area being but a little more than 23 square miles instead of the 36 square miles which constitute a regularly surveyed township. The Mattawamkeag River flows across the town from east to west, passing along the south front of Kingman Village and receiving various tributaries from the north and south before it leaves the town. The most important of these is the Molunkus Stream, which enters from Macwahoc at the northwest corner of Kingman, makes a slight curve which crosses and re-crosses the Mattawamkeag line, and then the course of the stream is straight and broad to its point of junction with the Mattawamkeag River, half a mile before it leaves the town. The Maine Central Railroad runs along near the north bank of this river in crossing Kingman, and the only regular station in town is at Kingman Village, which lies a little to the west and south of the centre of the township.

Several roads extend from the village, notably one following along the course of Molunkus Stream up into Macwahoc, for on the east side of this road the bulk of Kingman's population, exclusive of that at the village, is located, and a daily stage line is run from Macwahoc, Kingman village being the terminus of the route. The village has a long and narrow site along the north bank of the Mattawamkeag and contains not only the great majority of the population of the town but also its factories, stores, etc., Kingman village being really the town of Kingman to all intents and purposes. The great tannery turns out an enormous amount of sole leather annually, and the other products of the town include long and short lumber, harnesses, smith work, etc. There are several well stocked and ably managed stores, a hotel and other establishments for the accommodation of the public, and the educational facilities are very good considering the resources of the community and the attending conditions. The local associations include a society of the Independent Order of Good Templars, a juvenile branch of the same organization, and a lodge of the Ancient Order of United Workmen. The growth of Kingman is steady and sure although it seems slow in comparison to the development from 1870 to 1880, when the town far outstripped all others in the county in this respect, its population increasing more than three hundred per cent. But a marked increase in valuation is an even surer indication of prosperity than is an increase of population, and the fact that Kingman's estate valuation increased from $75,455.00 to $126,154.00 during the ten years from 1880 to 1890 shows that the town is making substantial progress and holds a prominent position among Maine's prosperous communities.

—

Representative Business Men Of Kingman.

WILBER GRANT,

MANUFACTURER OF

LUMBER.

Cedar Shingles, Clapboards, Lath, Etc.

Railroad Ties a Specialty.

KINGMAN. MAINE.

L. B. CLARK & CO., manufacturers "Kingman Hemlock Sole Leather Tannage," and dealers in General Merchandise, Kingman, Me.—One of the largest shoe manufacturers of Massachusetts said in a recent interview "No skins in the country furnish finer, more durable or more desirable sole stock than do those from the State of Maine," and those familiar with the reputation of the "Kingman Hemlock Sole Leather Tannage" need not be told that this town produces sole leather equal to any in the State and consequently unsurpassed by any produced in any section of the country. The tannery to which we have reference has a capacity of 3,000 hides per week and the industry is of the very first importance not only to this town but to all the region roundabout. The plant of machinery is of the most improved type and includes an engine of eighty horse-power. Employment is given to seventy-five experienced assistants and every process incidental to production is carefully supervised, no pains being spared to maintain the high reputation the "Kingman Hemlock Sole Leather Tannage," has for uniform and unsurpassed excellence. The business is carried on by Messrs. L. B. Clark & Co., who succeeded Messrs. F. S. Shaw & Brothers in 1885. The partners are Messrs. L. B. Clark and W. D. Shaw. The firm are very heavy dealers in general merchandise and carry an immense stock requiring the use of spacious storehouses as well as the occupancy of a warehouse containing two floors measuring 25×125 feet each. We need hardly add that the concern are in a position to quote bottom prices on goods of warranted quality, and to fill orders promptly.

B. F. OSGOOD, General Merchandise, Kingman, Me.—The more fully the establishment carried on by Mr. B. F. Osgood is investigated the more apparent does its popularity become and when the store is visited, the stock examined and the prices obtained, the investigator is obliged to confess that the popularity of the establishment is thoroughly well-deserved and that the residents of Kingman and vicinity know a good thing when they see it. This business was at one time conducted by Mr. W. S. Smith, who was succeeded by Mr. B. F. Osgood, jr., in 1887, the present owner assuming control in 1890. Mr. Osgood carries a very carefully chosen stock of groceries, dry goods, boots and shoes, clothing and other standard commodities, and guarantees every article he sells to prove just as represented. He caters expressly to family trade, depends upon regular and not on transient customers and so does his best to thoroughly satisfy every patron; and as we have before stated he succeeds so well in doing so that the enterprise with which he is identified is one of the most popular in this vicinity.

MRS. E. TRASK, Millinery and Fancy Goods, Books, Papers, etc., Kingman, Me.—The popularity of any store is of course dependent to a great extent upon the character of the stock carried, but this is particularly the case with a millinery store, for the very best management in other respects will be of no avail unless the goods in stock include late fashionable novelties and are so frequently renewed as always to be fresh and attractive. Mrs. E. Trask is well aware of this fact, if we may judge from the frequency with which her stock is renewed and the care with which it is chosen, at all events her assortment of millinery and fancy goods is always very attractive, and an "opening" at her store is always of great interest to the ladies of this vicinity. She deals in books, newspapers, etc., as well as in millinery and fancy goods, and this department of her business is of considerable importance and is steadily gaining in patronage. Mrs. Trask has been in business here about six years and has built up quite a large trade, but sufficient assistance is employed to ensure the prompt and careful filling of every order.

MRS. F. G. LEAVITT, General Merchandise, Kingman, Me.—There are very many "general stores" in this State, and the majority of them are well stocked, but few so thoroughly deserve the name of "general store," as does that conducted by Mrs. E. G. Leavitt, for few can show so large an assortment of goods, as our readers will agree when they learn that among the more important articles dealt in by Mrs. Leavitt are groceries, dry and fancy goods, boots and shoes, tinware, wall paper, window shades, jewelry, canned goods, meats and fish, and millinery goods, a specialty being made of fine millinery work to order. Spacious premises are occupied and the stock is constantly being renewed, so that it is always complete in every department and includes the latest and most popular novelties. The business was founded in 1870, by Mr. Almon Leavitt, and has been carried on by Mrs. Leavitt since 1880. It is very efficiently managed, and sufficient assistance is employed to ensure prompt and careful attention to every customer.

INDEX TO BUSINESS NOTICES.